MW00616457

WHY ME?

Other Books by Arleen Lorrance

THE LOVE PROJECT

CHANNELING LOVE ENERGY
(with Diane K. Pike)

BUDDHA FROM BROOKLYN

MUSINGS FOR MEDITATION

WHY ME?

How to Heal What's Hurting You

Arleen Lorrance

Rawson Associates Publishers, Inc.
New York

Library of Congress Cataloging in Publication Data
Lorrance, Arleen
Why me?
Bibliography: p.
Includes index.
1. Conduct of life. I. Title.
BJ1581.2.L695 158'.1 77-88151
ISBN 0-89256-038-X

Published simultaneously in Canada by
McClelland and Stewart, Ltd.
Manufactured in the United States of America
by Fairfield Graphics, Fairfield, Pennsylvania
Designed by Gene Siegel
Second Printing June 1978

For BEBE KAPLAN . . .
a friend who loves me unconditionally
who is always there when needed
who helped me to heal myself by
making me do all the work!

For MILLIE BOUCHER . . .
who had painful occasion to ask
Why Me? and answered herself by
becoming a radiant and whole person.

And for MR. & MRS. MANUEL MACHADO . .
my very dear neighbors who inspired this
book by being willing to share a life
crisis and their tears with me.

ACKNOWLEDGMENTS

I would especially like to thank the Universe through which this material was channeled; Diane Kennedy Pike, my Spiritual Friend and colleague, who mirrors JOY for me as well as being an equal pillar with me in our Work and whose suggestions, editorial help, and encouragement were invaluable; thousands of *Seekers* throughout the world who practiced beside me in five years of sessions during which much of the material in this book was being applied and refined; Gertrude Platt and Ann Dunagan for their help in preparing the manuscript; Dr. Sy Cutler who helped me through six months of heart disease by prescribing that I be healed without medication or hospitalization since nature must take its course; my mother, Rose Udoff, who worries about me so that I don't have to; my father, Irving Udoff, who taught me to be a scrapper and to love myself; Eleanor Rawson, my publisher, who read the manuscript, who rejoiced in its worth, who said YES, who wanted to make it available to those in pain in order that they might heal themselves, my Higher Self which guides my life in wondrous perfection and had wisdom enough to channel the contents of this book.

CONTENTS

INTRODUCTION

Before I say anything else, let me tell you that I love you. My love for you is not some phony, sticky, sentimental love. It doesn't come from a once-removed author to a generalized reader. My love for you is my way of reawakening and reactivating your love for yourself. I love you in *your* name—especially during this, your time of suffering, when you may not be loving yourself very much.

I love you *because* you are struggling, faltering, feeling insecure. This means that you are growing; I love growth. It also means that you are capable of handling the crisis you've been given to deal with. I *know* that, because you wouldn't have been stricken if you weren't ready to handle it. You may not think you are ready, but you are. I love you for being able. I love you for thinking that you're not. I may not be feeling your pain or suffering your exact trouble, but I have felt my own, suffered my own, and because I have, I can commiserate with you

Who am I? Someone who has discovered how to

set healing energy in motion and can show *you* how to do it. I am someone who was stricken and made it . . . made it not only in terms of continuing to live, but in terms of learning some very important life lessons in the midst of a very serious dis-ease. It would have been easier to learn them *after* the time of crisis. It's always easier to look back and reflect from a vantage point of comfort. You can boast to your friends and show off your scars—physical or emotional. The hard part is to be able to reflect while in the midst of the struggle. Although it may be hard, it is vital to the healing process.

That's why I'm writing this for you. I've been in your place. I enabled myself to be healed with no apparent scars. I want to provide you with the opportunity to begin your healing. That is, if you *want* to. Wanting to is critical.

This book is for you no matter what you've been stricken with—heart disease, addictions, mental illness, bad luck, cancer, failure in school, loss of a loved one, rape, paralysis, job loss, broken bones, acne, desperation, a stroke, depression, etc. It's not the specific condition that's important; it's that you *have* a condition, that (as you see it) *it happened to you.*

Your condition, be it a state of pain, of hurting, of trouble, or a time of crisis, is causing you to suffer dis-ease: an active disharmony that has thrown your life into upheaval. The disharmony can be physical, mental, emotional, spiritual, or any combination of these. It is in relation to all of these, and therefore to you if you are so afflicted, that this book is directed.

"Why me?" is an appropriate question. After all, it's unfair. You don't want to be here. You don't belong in this mess. You want out. You want this thing to go away. "Why me?" is a question to scream loudly and often. It's OK to ask it, and you are the only one who can answer it.

If all you do is *ask* the question, you make yourself a victim. If you want to *be* a victim, then don't read any further. But if you are ready to move beyond being a victim, then move beyond *asking,* "Why me?" to *answering* that question, and you will begin to activate the healing process. It's up to you.

Who am I? Your helper. I'm your bedside companion, your alter-ego, the echo of your inner voice. I'll stay with you long after all your friends, family, and visitors are gone. I'll be beside you when you are alone with the ravagings of your own hopelessness. I'll comfort you, but I'll challenge you too! I won't let you get away with anything. However, you are in charge. It's your illness, your trouble, your condition, your agony. Anytime you don't want to cope, all you have to do is put me down, close my pages. I won't "put you down" for putting me down. Wanting to feel sorry for yourself, wanting to give up or to suffer more, can be a very important part of the healing process.

Who am I? A person just like you. I hurt, I cry, I struggle. I've had, and have not ceased to have, crises with which to deal. That's the life process. I've been disappointed in relationships. I've suffered heart disease. I've thought of myself as stupid, as a failure. I've grieved over death snatching a loved one. I've had times of disconnecting from what is called reality and wondering if I were going off the deep end.

If life is heavy for you right now, I'm someone who knows what heaviness is.

Who am I? A person just like you. I am capable of healing myself. I am rich in inner strength ready to be drawn upon. I am someone who knows joy, even if it seems in the distant past right now.

Being able to activate healing, to call upon inner strength, to reexperience joy, *especially* now in the midst of the pain, is a matter of being able to hear your own Higher voice speaking to you. That voice is a voice of clarity which rings with truth in the midst of what seems like static. The static *is* there. So is the voice of clarity.

I will be a reflection of that voice for you. *Your* voice speaking to you through the static. My voice *is* your voice, if what I say speaks to you. It is the Higher Self you've known so many times before (before this time of pain) and will know again.

As personalities, you and I are no doubt very different. In Higher Self, in that voice of clarity, you and I are *no* different. We have the same power to take ourselves up into our own hands and guide ourselves through the trouble of now.

Who am I? Someone who has been practicing lifting myself for many years through many trials. I found my way with the help of my own Higher

Self and six simple principles known as The Love Project. The principles are:

Receive all persons as beautiful exactly where they are.

Create your own reality consciously, rather than living as if you have no control over your life.

Have no expectations, but rather abundant expectancy.

Be the change you want to see happen, instead of trying to change everyone else.

Provide others with the opportunity to give.

Perceive problems as opportunities.

These principles were given to me, channeled through me, in 1970, following an awakening to the consciousness that I was all there was *and* nothing, all at the same time. It was then that I made the choice to be totally loving, open, and vulnerable. It was these principles that enabled me to activate my clear voice and they continue to help me to do so. Throughout our time together, we will explore these principles and see how they might be helpful to you.

Who am I? I am a mirror of the part of you that affirms yourself. I invite you to look in the mirror of me to see your wholeness.

I am an example that you can survive, can walk tall, can smile—long after what's hurting you has moved on. I'm not wiser than you. I represent the wiseness *in* you. I'm your reminder of the more that you are.

I will serve as a friend who has learned to function out of Higher Self by sharing with you my own life experiences and showing you how I pulled myself through times of suffering. Simultaneously, I will be inviting you to activate your own Higher Self and to apply the explorations and steps offered to pulling yourself up out of the pain that envelops you.

Who am I? I am one who knows that you can get well if you want to. I'm here at your side with the next step if you're ready for me.

WHY ME?

1

THE IMPACT OF THE DIS-EASE ITSELF

"WHY ME??!!" Have you shouted it as much as you want to? If you haven't, go right ahead. I'm with you one hundred percent. I really mean it. I don't see you as any less of a person if you shake your fists, grind your teeth, stamp your feet, pound the wall, shout "Why me?" at the top of your lungs. I love you for it. I see you as *more* of a person. I see you as someone who is hurting, who has a burgeoning well of feelings and who is letting those feelings flow. Hallelujah! You're letting them flow. Do it if you haven't. Do it as often as you need to. Shout the words so the whole universe will hear you.

"WHY ME?! I don't bother anyone. I can think of at least twenty people who deserve this more than I do. They are mean and nasty. They make everyone around them feel miserable. Why not them? Why me?" *Or,* "Why me? Haven't I suffered enough?

It's their turn now! After all, there's only so much one person can bear."

Say it in all the words that are meaningful to you. Say it with all your heart. After you've let it out, you'll feel freer, easier, perhaps even spent. For the words "Why me?" are actually frantic attempts to express the intense feelings you have about your condition. Your feelings need to be expressed. The question "Why me?" is one way of letting those feelings out.

"Why me? I work hard. I apply myself. I don't shirk my responsibility. How come this never strikes the shiftless of the world? Why me?"

Perhaps you are wanting to shout something else. Something like, "Why me? How come I was singled out to suffer?" *Or,* "Why me? I didn't do anything to deserve this."

Keep shouting "Why me?" until the energy of the feelings begins to change. You will feel the difference. In the beginning the words are shouted out of anger—as a way of lashing out at the world and the condition itself. Sometimes they also express frustration at your seeming helplessness in the face of the circumstances in which you find yourself.

But if you keep asking the question, you may find it turning to anguish. In the anquish lies a genuine cry for help. When "Why me?" expresses the full intensity of your pain and suffering, then it ceases to be rhetorical and becomes a genuine question.

To "Why me?" asked in anger or frustration,

there is no answer because none is yet being sought. To "Why me?" asked in anguish or in true searching, there *are* answers, for in the question lies the open door to new understanding.

If you are *really* asking "Why me?" I'll help you to answer that question and to get on with your life.

Let's begin with what *seems* like the hardest part—the condition itself. You don't want to focus on it, do you? I don't blame you. Who wants to think about something that's ruined their life? It has, you know. You may never be the same, *if* you come through this. You may not be able to function normally. You may be handicapped. You may be half the person you were. Damn, you may be dead!

Have thoughts like this been going through your head? Have you been beating yourself up with them, torturing yourself and thus making yourself even sicker? If you have, stop for a minute. I'd like to give you a new perspective on what you've been doing.

First, I want you to notice that all the questions I've asked you have to do with what *you* are doing to *yourself*. It's not the dis-ease that is suggesting to you that you'll never get well. It's *you* who are suggesting that to *yourself*.

This may surprise you, but "you" and "yourself" are not necessarily one and the same. That's why you can suggest things to yourself. There are many facets to your being: your rational mind (or re-mind), your feeling self (or little self), your physical body, and your Higher Self, to mention four.

Your rational mind is the center where all your thoughts and questions are stored. That's why I call it your re-mind. It feeds back whatever you've learned and recorded. It is your imprint center. Every life experience is stamped there in an orderly, naturally-computerized system. Your re-mind includes the faculties of intellect and reasoning. The re-mind always wants to understand what's happening to you. It constantly asks why, or more pointedly, "Why me?" The re-mind often provides a very acceptable *understanding* for the condition you might have and yet has no impact whatsoever on the condition itself. For example, if you were fired from your job, your re-mind might explain it by telling you:

a. You simply were not appreciated
b. It wasn't your fault
c. Your boss was a rat-fink S.O.B.

While such analysis explains what happens in a way that seems to satisfy your intellectual perception of the situation, it does nothing to deal with your *feelings* of hurt and abandonment, your sense of insecurity, your need and want to have a job, your pride.

If you'd like to, take a moment and look into your rational mind. What does it think about your condition? What is it telling you about yourself? Is it being hard on you? Or rather, are you being hard on yourself through the thoughts you are directing your way? Do you *think* things should be going differently for you and are you therefore *upset* that they aren't? Upset is rooted in lopsidedness. You are lopsided if your re-mind has taken over and is running the entire show. Your feelings want to be expressed but your rational mind has closed them out. The result: you are upset, off-balance.

Your re-mind has important data to offer you, and it is valuable as long as you register it in the context of your feelings and intuitions (from your Higher Self) so that you achieve a balance.

Thought	***Feeling***	***Intuition***
I wasn't appreciated	I'm hurt by that	I can find others who will appreciate me
It wasn't my fault	I'm always picked on	I may be setting myself up as a fall guy
My boss is a rat-fink S.O.B.	I want to throw him against a wall and jump up and down on him	Whatever he is has nothing to do with who I am and my worth as a person

Moving from thought to feeling to intuition is a fine pathway for setting healing energy in motion.

When you limit yourself to your re-mind alone, you limit your possibilities.

Another thing about the re-mind is that more often than not when you are feeling miserable, the data it brings forth is the worst news it can think of. Conversely, when you are feeling great, your re-mind offers you one terrific thought after another. But you can take charge of what the re-mind calls up. When you're feeling low, ask it for good news and when you're feeling great, ask it for confirmation of that.

Your re-mind has a direct influence on the other facets of your being—your little self and your body. When your re-mind tells you that you'll never make it through this, it's your feeling self, your little self, that suffers the fear, the hurt, the anxiety. It is important to be conscious of that process of interaction so that you can direct it.

Mind you I am not advocating that you cease thinking "negative" thoughts and produce only "positive" ones. I am simply inviting you to become aware of your rational mind, to be alert to the fact that it is thinking, that it is offering you those thoughts. Once you know that, you will no longer be the prisoner of your own thoughts, you will be a choice-maker in relation to them. You will be the liberator of your feeling self, your little self, who is the direct victim of incriminating thought patterns.

Your little self is associated with your solar plexus, where you experience feelings. It is a tender part of yourself. Your little self is the child you once were, still are, and always will be. That child, that little self of you, resides within you, sometimes frightened, often wide-eyed with awe at all there is in the universe. Your little self wants and needs love and affection from others and from you. Whether or not you receive that love depends on how willing you are to ask for it, how much you choose to receive, how secure you feel about being exposed to the risk.

Your feelings *will not* be ignored. They persist, even though your rational mind may *think* you should not have them.

A case in point is the condition of grief. Your rational mind might well be in a hurry to end the suffering process. Hence, it might offer you the thoughts, "You've wept enough. Crying won't bring the person back. Forget it. You're an adult. Start acting like one." These thoughts might be fine for your rational mind but your little self may *not* have wept enough. The feelings may be so full in you that you need to cry for months in order to empty the well. Thoughts can be forgotten. Feelings must be felt and experienced. It is true that your rational mind is the intellectual part of yourself, yet the child or little self is equally important. All facets of yourself are given to you in order that you might honor them equally and experience them fully.

The conflict between your doomsday-predicting re-mind and your victimized little self is manifested in tension and in pain in your physical body. It is your physical body which bears the brunt of the engagement. This is how you beat up on yourself. Your re-mind lashes out in attacks, your little self experiences the thought-blows as hurt feelings and your body gives form to both in a dis-ease.

Let's look at a specific instance of how this process might work. As an accident-prone person, you have developed a mind-set that you and trouble are magnetized to one another. You may not realize that you have, and so in your unawareness you get hurt and constantly ask, "Why me?" You have yourself programmed to unite with areas of danger and to be blind to them. In part you've done this by recording in your re-mind the fact that you are prone to accidents. Hence, if there is a rusty nail, you will be sure to be barefoot, you will be sure not to see it, you will be sure to step on it. Immediately your re-mind takes it out on your little self. "Why don't you watch where you are going? Why don't you wear shoes? Why are you so stupid? Why can't you take care of yourself?" (The re-mind loves to ask "why" questions.)

Little self feels terrible—helpless, hopeless, dumb. Little self withdraws, resorts to shallow breathing (thus hindering the healing process), and pouts. Simultaneously, the body registers the signs of the dis-ease. The wound is festering and hurting. Blame intensifies the pain of it. Hurt feelings complicate the experience and divert energies from the healing of the wound itself.

You can monitor the entire process and make some new choices if you will plug into your Higher

Self. This is the self with which you see the whole and in which you remain detached, even in the midst of experiencing.

Your Higher Self is your God-Self. It is the self through which you express love unconditionally. The Higher Self is your center of knowing, of intuition. You don't think or feel in Higher Self, you simply know. You are *sure* even though you can't say why. Your Higher Self is the mediator, the harmonizer, that brings balance to your life.

Take the example of you as an accident-prone person. Your Higher Self might immediately embrace you in your pain, indicate what steps are necessary to be taken immediately (washing the wound, getting a tetanus shot, etc.), and invite you to look at how this fits in with larger patterns in your life in which you engage in hurting yourself.

Your Higher Self serves as a monitor, a nonjudgmental observer of what is transpiring in the various facets of yourself. It enables you to bring thoughts, feelings, and bodily sensations into balance as a cohesive whole.

Speaking in general terms, your Higher Self allows you to take charge, to pull your life back into order when you begin to feel yourself coming loose at the seams. For example, every time your re-mind asks, "What if?" tell it to cool it. There isn't any way to deal with "What if?" It means nothing. When your re-mind asks, "What if?" your Higher Self can direct the re-mind to answer itself by calling up the data it has to work with right now: "My heartbeat is irregular," "I have no feeling in my legs," "I can't cope," "I can't get my memory to function," "I'm in a deep hole of depression." State whatever *is* the condition of right now, period.

Then, lest your little self be frightened that what is *now* will *always* be so, be loving to that part of yourself. Acknowledge that it would be terrible if the effects of now were to remain forever, but recharge yourself with the fact that you have no way of knowing that. It might get better. It might get worse. Worst of all are "mights." They go nowhere.

The best way to look to the future is to live totally in the now. Tomorrow hasn't happened yet. Trying to live tomorrow today is frustrating because it can never be accomplished.

This much you know today: You don't want what you've been stricken with. I hear you. I don't want it for you either. However, what good does your not wanting it do for you? It doesn't make it go away. It doesn't heal it.

To not want is a state of inactivity, and therefore a continuance of where you are.

Would you like to practice? I'm right here beside you to help if you'd like to look at some of your feelings and move past some of your don't wants.

Ask yourself what your feeling is about your state of being. If nasty words present themselves as descriptions, feel free to put them down. No one is going to mark your paper. If you have fears of what might happen, list them, and right next to them list what's happening in reality. An example might be:

Fear	***Reality***
I'll never walk again	I can't walk right now
I'll never get over this	I'm having trouble coping

Use your own specifics. Do you see what this does? It brings the *truth* into focus and takes you past supposition. It makes your situation clearer, more manageable. I want that for you. You deserve that much, and much more.

Want to do a little more? Check out your "don't wants." Write them all down. "I don't want ———." Make as long a list as you need to. Then go back, and next to each one write, "Instead, I want ———." See what you come up with. When you talk about these problems in the future, speak of what you *do* want rather than what you don't. Then you will set the healing energy in motion. Try it and see. Not for me. Do it for you. Do it because we both care about you.

Where do you go from here?

Your re-mind may tell you that you should fight against your condition. Your relatives and friends may encourage the same course of action. "Don't give in. Don't give up. Fight it. You can win." The advice is interesting, but how would you go about it? The dis-ease is yours. It's living in *you*. How do you go to war against yourself, and win, without also losing? Furthermore, when you are in a weak and vulnerable state, where do you get the energy to go into battle? And since when can you bring harmony into being by creating anti-energy and attacking? Surely it can make you tired just to think of it.

Rest a minute, my friend. Breathe deeply and rest. Close your eyes, put this book down and simply lie in stillness.

Let's forget about fighting. It doesn't work. Let's look again at where you are. A deep sigh would be helpful right now. You still have the condition. It hasn't gone away. You still don't want it, even though you know that not wanting it won't help. How's your little self just now? Are you feeling hopeless, feeling sorry for yourself? Are you biting your lower lip, or grinding your teeth? Are there tears in your eyes? Well, my dear one, if you want to cry, do it. I'll wait for you. Crying is healthy. It keeps your channels open so that energy can keep flowing in. You need that energy for healing. Whenever you have a feeling, *feel* it. Don't push it aside. Feelings are just like your condition. They won't go away either. They are *your* feelings. You can't ignore them as if they were strangers invading your life-space. They were born in you. They'll move on only when you have felt them, experienced them, not before.

This is a very important point. Surely you've heard this illness-related expression, "It has to run its course." Feelings, too, have to run their courses.

Everything has its time, its size, and its shape. When you create something (when you bring it into being), be it a feeling, an idea, a way of life, a problem, a habit, it has a specific configuration. It occupies a definite time and space. Once it has been brought into being it does not vanish simply because you don't want it any more. To be totally through with something, you need to move totally through it. You can't run away from it because it will remain. It will wait for you, cropping up again and again until you meet it face to face, move into it, embrace it, know its energy, move that energy into a new form and thus move through it to the new. Then you will be finished.

Feelings are not haphazard occurrences. They are the vehicles through which you respond to yourself and your world. They are the soul's way of cleansing your body and your being of decay-producing residue. When you let your tears flow, you wash the windows of the house of your inner wisdom. They become clean so that you can look into them and see what next steps you can take in your present crisis.

If you're not too tired, let's focus again on your condition. Whatever you are stricken with, one thing is for sure. Your condition is the *end* of a way of being. That's the way it is with problems. A problem is an opportunity to begin living and functioning differently. It's important for you to acknowledge that.

I'm talking to your Higher Self. I'm not asking

you to accept it or be happy about it. Nor am I asking you to argue about it or deny it. Just acknowledge it. Recognize the truth of it. Say it is so.

You will never be the same as you were. Are you breathing? Breathe deeply and say it like it is. From this day forth you will be different. *You will be new.* You don't know *how* you will be different from what you were, you know only that you *will* be, that you are.

Check out what you are doing right now. What kind of data are you calling up from your re-mind? Are you beating up yourself again? Are you telling yourself that if you can't be the same as you were, you can only be worse than you were? There is at least one other possibility, you know. You might well turn out to be far better than you ever were! Whenever you call up gloom, at least leave room for the opposite as well. Then, let go of all data about the future and acknowledge the facts of now. "I am not what I was. I am different. I am emerging new. I don't know what that new is yet."

If you can say yes to this truth, without thinking the worst or calling up fear, you can get on with living.

What you're saying yes to is nothing unusual. The fact is that before you were stricken, every day of your life was an end of one way of being and each new day was the beginning of a new one. You feel it more now because it's more intense, more concentrated. Hence, it is brought more sharply into your consciousness. You've been shouted at by life, instead of being communicated with in the whispers to which you are accustomed. Don't be intimidated by the volume. Listen more intently and you'll modulate yourself into perfect harmony. Prior to this, life circumstances merely asked you to listen. This condition is *demanding* your attention. That's why you now experience it as an imposition, as a *profound* end to your former way of life. It struck like an earthquake. You weren't ready.

Know this, my friend: only where there are profound endings are there profound new beginnings.

Life shouted at you, threw you down flat. Now, you are being asked to find a new center of balance. Your Higher Self is calling you—inviting you to take control, asking you to unite the facets of yourself, offering you the opportunity to activate the energy of healing and to make whole the fragments that are causing you to suffer. Your Higher Self is calling you. I can help you to hear it.

2

YESTERDAY: THE BEGINNING WHICH LED TO THE RESULT OF TODAY

In the introduction, I told you I loved you. I told you I was your friend. In addition to being gentle with you, I told you I was going to challenge you. That's what I'd like to do now—to challenge you. By this I mean I'd like to stimulate you to see if, by any chance, you directly or indirectly participated in bringing your current state of being into reality.

What I say might not be true of you If that is so, let it go. But it *may* apply to you. If it does, and if you are willing to admit that it does, this may be one of the most important chapters for you.

Before we begin, let me acknowledge something to you. If you find that I'm describing *you* in these pages and you don't like what I'm saying, your feelings may get hurt. Your little self may want to say, "I don't like you anymore," or, "Go to the devil." Your rational mind might jump in with thoughts like, "Who do you think you are, saying things like this to me?" Your body may wince in pain if I strike the right chord.

If you want to jump all over me, go right ahead. What I'm about to propose is very nitty-gritty material. It could be a blow to your ego. This will be especially true if you believe that what's wrong with you is the fault of someone or something other than yourself.

If you still want and need the comfort of thinking that you are not responsible, I support you in your continuance of that. You may never see anything other than that as a possibility. That is equally as beautiful as being willing to explore your participation in the creation of the dis-ease.

I am not speaking with the voice of a rational mind. I do not, nor will I ever, pass judgment on you. I am speaking as the voice of a Higher Self. I love and respect you, unconditionally. I receive you in your perfection no matter *where* you are in your present state, or what you think or feel.

As you read, I encourage you to read from the vantage point of Higher Self, to open yourself to new possibilities. Shout at me if you want to but at least be honest with yourself and acknowledge which facet of your being is doing the shouting.

If you are ready, take a deep breath and let's begin.

If you are to have a tomorrow, it's important for you to look straight into the eye of yesterday.

Yesterday is how you got to where you are today. You may not remember what you did in all the yesterdays that led to your being stricken. I wasn't even there but I *know* something of what you did. *You participated in the creation of your dis-ease,* that is what you did. You can argue with me about that if you like. You can tell me, "It came out of the blue." Or, "It just happened to me," or "I didn't want it; I didn't ask for it. I didn't do anything to get it. Pow! It simply struck." If you want to add anything else, go right ahead. I won't argue with you, though. You see, I *know* that *you* helped do it. Your arguing with me to prove otherwise is simply wasted energy. However, this much I will acknowledge. You participated in the creation of this dis-ease, but you were perhaps *unaware* that you did so. Can you acknowledge that much?

I'm not engaging in a contest with you. I'm not *asking* you to affirm my perception. I *am* asking you to open yourself to the possibility that you bear a degree of responsibility for what you now have. There is a bonus attached if you will acknowledge that much. The bonus is the possibility of getting well faster and more fully. You see, if you will affirm that even though you may not have been aware of doing so, you took part in the creation of your condition, you can also affirm your ability to have a hand in creating a new one!

If you're with me thus far, I want to take this one step further. You are a creative person. Perhaps you never thought of yourself that way but you are. You have created a piece worthy of display in any life museum which handles exhibits on the human condition. An artist's creativity is often measured by the worth of the finished product. By such standards, your creativity would depend on the depth and intensity of the dis-ease you have brought into being. Simply stated, the sicker you are, the more hopeless you feel, the more impossible the outlook for the future, the greater the indication of your talent.

Now, to the more important point. The greater your gift for helping to create the dis-ease, the greater your potential for helping to heal yourself, for moving beyond where you are now, for bringing into being new healthfulness and greater harmony.

Let's take a look into the yesterdays in which your creational process occurred. Who were you? What were your priorities? How much did you consider the whole of yourself? Were you investing so much energy in an idea, a wish, a goal, a desire—an outer task—that you neglected to draw life energy into all the facets of yourself?

Your little self may have longed for play time or needed affection. You may have left no time for fully loving another or being loved in return.

Your body may have needed to touch, to be touched. It may have needed to be nourished and cared for.

What of your rational mind? Did you provide it with new stimulation, with exercise outlets for its faculties? Perhaps you never gave it any rest, any quiet. Perhaps you overworked it, made demands on it.

And where was your Higher Self in the midst of

those yesterdays? Were you acknowledging your intuitions? Were you choosing to be and to do all that you knew to be true? Or were you compromising your values? Perhaps you neglected to open yourself to meditative stillness, to the higher, finer vibrations. To allow little or no spiritual input into your life is to leave your body unattended, at the mercy of the elements or the elemental forces.

If you indeed left these facets of yourself devoid of the input they needed, is it any wonder that they crowded in on you by manifesting a dis-ease or a situation with which to attack you, to demand your attention? Can you see how this is tantamount to participating in the creation of the reality of crisis for yourself?

Did you hold an important title or significant job? More to the point, was your title or job important to you? Were you on a forced march to the pinnacle known as success? Were you *too busy* being outer directed to also be inner directed? Were you so into your work that you lost yourself in an all-encompassing goal?

Perhaps you felt the opposite about your job. Perhaps you hated it or were bored with it. You wanted out. Did you get out? No? Is that the reason for being stricken? If it was, then you *did* get out, the hard way. For example, were you hit by a car? You know the scene. You're simply crossing the street, minding your own business and out of nowhere the machine barrels down on you and puts you in the hospital. It wasn't your fault. It was pure accident. Well, *maybe* it was. As you lie in the hospital room with your leg in a cast and in traction, a thought crosses your mind. You are having a much needed rest and collecting sick pay. You aren't having to work. You're free. You might even get an insurance settlement which would provide the security you need to give you time to look for another job.

Now I'm not saying you planned it this way. But you *did* want out of your job and now you *are* out. The breaking of your leg is the symbolic representation of the break with your job.

There are many other ways to do it: create an ulcer, get pregnant even though you don't want another child, downgrade your work performance so that you are fired, create a nervous disorder that forces you to be homebound. The possibilities are endless, and all of them are in some way hurtful to the self.

If you take one of these routes, you get out of the job all right, the hard way. It's like jumping out of a plane without a parachute. It's effective. It frees you. The only trouble is, you have very little control over where and how you land. There was an alternative way of creating the reality. You simply might have quit.

You were doing something yesterday. What was it? What was it that brought you to the pain you're in now?

Perhaps you wanted out of or into a relationship. Creating severe dis-ease for yourself is a very dramatic way of accomplishing the task—that is, if you're still around long enough to partake of any of the resultant fruits.

Were you treading water in a sea of aimlessness, your course without purpose or direction, your sails flapping without care at the mercy of the wind? Did you simply decide to sink?

Was it that you were unworthy? Is that what you were feeling in your lifetime of yesterdays? Did you not deserve to be well, to be joyful, to be whole? When you were little did someone tell you that you were born bad, that you were no good? Did you believe it? Did you spend yesterday convincing yourself that since you were basically rotten, the wrath of some terrible force was supposed to fall on your head? If you did all this, you did it well. The proof is your current state, your bad luck, your sorrowful condition. After all, you thoroughly convinced yourself that you weren't worthy of anything more!

You may have poured out the telltale signs of your unworthiness daily with little phrases like, "I'll never get a promotion. I'm not good enough." "I'll never get that raise. After all, who am I?" "My marriage probably won't last very long. My mate will tire of me." "I'll probably never marry. I'm nothing special." "Don't say nice things about me. They're not true." (Fill in your own. If you feel unworthy, you no doubt have a very long list that covers a wide variety of possibilities. I couldn't even begin to know all the items that you know to be wrong with you.) Be specific. How did you proclaim your unworthiness in the wealth of yesterdays prior to creating your dis-ease?

Maybe it wasn't unworthiness. Perhaps you were unconscious in relation to your everyday life. You did your chores, related to your relatives, were friendly with your friends. Perhaps you, more than anyone else, are asking the question, "Why me?" After all, you didn't *do* anything! *There* may be your answer. You were doing nothing—you were going through the motions of life rather than living it. You were exposed to the bumps and scrapes of life without being aware that you were one-half of a partnership. You were walloped because you walked directly into an outstretched fist and never saw it until you allowed yourself to feel it. When you don't live life in a consciously-directed manner, life lives through you haphazardly. When you don't step out with specific intent, you leave yourself open to tripping, to being stricken.

Perhaps, as in the example of the auto incident, you ended up with broken bones in order to break with the past. You refused to do it for yourself in a conscious way, so your body did it *for* you. Or rather, you did it for yourself by unconsciously doing it to your body. Case in point: if you were tired of meeting a long-standing obligation to care for an aging parent who lived nearby, you might have broken a strategic bone which disabled you from driving. Thus, someone else would have had to take up the task and you, while saving face, would at last have broken away from the cross you had to bear. Another example: if you were tired of cooking for your family every day and night, did you sprain your wrist to get out of doing it, instead of *asking* others to share in the responsibility? Of course, there are other effective ways of "breaking out," especially out of the kitchen. Develop an allergy; break out in a rash. You can't possibly go on cooking under those conditions. If it only gets you out of cooking certain foods, extend it to a greater variety of dishes. You may not be able to eat much as a result, but you *will* have gotten free of a task you no longer want to perform.

How are you doing? Are you breathing? Are we still friends? Do you think I'm accusing you? I'm not. If that's what your mind *thinks,* here's an opportunity for you to observe your mind in action. Acknowledge what your mind is thinking and move beyond those thoughts to what we are actually doing together. We're looking into what might have led to where you are today. That's all we're doing. No accusations. Just look.

How about your little self? Is she or he feeling threatened or frightened? Assure your little self that there will be no punishment if you discover that you were doing something to bring disharmony into being. Rather, it will be a time for rejoicing. To discover what you did then and no longer want to do in the future, is to be able to make new choices in the now. That's pure joy, new freedom, wondrous release.

Assure your little self. Embrace yourself with love as you continue exploring.

Let's look at another possibility in the answer box of yesterday. Was it that you stopped living by settling unhappily for what you had in life, and brought hardening of the arteries or stiffness of the joints into being? To settle is to congeal in place, like jello: you become part of the mold into which you've poured and locked yourself. There's no way out. You grow moldy after a time. Dis-ease sets in.

If you settled, you gave up. You dropped yourself into quicksand and began to sink very rapidly, precipitating the crisis with which you are now dealing.

If you settled, you had plenty of ways to rationalize your actions. "I'll never get a better job so I might as well stay with this one until I retire. At least I'll get a pension out of it." There it is! An open invitation to dis-ease. Your system will not tolerate stagnation. Preparing for years-from-now while being unsatisfied by every moment of the present, is to die now in order to live later. It can't be done, at least not harmoniously.

Maybe the way you settled was in relation to your marriage. Sometimes couples who stay together work out more of a settlement than those who divorce. What about it? Did you settle for companionship because you didn't trust that you'd ever find the mate you were really looking for? Did you sacrifice so as not to be lonely and then find yourself being lonelier than ever when you were in the company of the other? Were you willing to let the deep love you dreamed about go, in order to have steady sex and a family to belong to?

Did you settle for being less than you could have been because you were too lazy to pip the shell you used to cover over your aspirations?

Perhaps you gave less of yourself than you were able, loved less, did not open yourself to new possibilities in your relationship. Perhaps you resisted change in your partner.

If you settled in any way, in relation to anything, you stirred dis-ease within you.

I don't know your exact situation, your hidden goal, the specific configuration of your life, but *you* do. For some reason you may have made the choice to bring into being the reality you are in now. Find it. Reveal it to yourself and you'll get in touch with the real dis-ease you have.

What you're suffering from now may not necessarily be the dis-ease. It may be the visible, manifested symptom of the actual dis-ease—the symptom which is treatable by doctors, soothable by counselors, or is labeled incurable by all concerned.

The actual dis-ease resides in the disharmony you encouraged in the energy forces moving through your being. There are many ways you might have done this. You may have put up barriers to the inflow and blocked the outflow. For example, you may have inhaled breath in a very shallow fashion, hence not providing enough fuel to efficiently carry you through the tasks you set for yourself. Your exhaling may have been limited, weak. *Because* you never took in enough, you never *had* enough to send back into the world. What you give is what you receive. A weak cycle of giving and receiving results in a fragile interaction with life. If the dis-ease took up residence in your lungs, your body may be making a very clear statement about how you participate in this give and take process.

Or, you may have twisted the lines of your own communications system. When someone called on you to give, you may have viewed it as an imposition rather than as an opportunity, thus creating tension, and withholding where release and letting flow were actually called for.

When a loved one said "No," to you, you may have received that "No" as that person's way of hurting you, rather than as a way of being honest with you and *therefore* loving you. You may have so hurt yourself in that loved one's name that you metaphorically fell apart and into your present crisis.

Of course, something else may have happened yesterday. Something entirely different. Until now we've spent a lot of time focusing on what you might have neglected to do which resulted in this present state, and on what you may have done that you would no longer want to do, now that you are conscious of it.

I've talked about these two approaches at length primarily because they are two major ways in which dis-ease comes into being.

Lest you think that only if you do something negative does something terrible come into being, let me propose another possibility to you.

You may have helped to create your current

state because you were finished with the phase of life in which you were living all those yesterdays. When you are ready for a radical evolutionary thrust in your soul growth, a revolutionary end to the old is called for. The end of one life brings the beginning of another, and in this case, it's all taking place in one body. Lightning strikes your status quo. You burn out the old wires because intuitively you know that they will be incapable of carrying the new vibrations with which you plan to charge them. Hence, you create the reality of dis-ease, or even near death. You take yourself out of action, out of the world in which you subjectively functioned and which you mistook for an objective reality. You put yourself into a hold pattern in the hope that you might slowly create the new.

In this case, you aren't doing anything "negative." Rather, you are stopping your old self through the means of some crisis and thus opening your new self to a next level of functioning for which you are fully ready.

For example, you may have had (given yourself) a heart attack. This is a sure way of stopping yourself. Prior to the attack, you may have been a good person, a loving mate, someone who was satisfied with life as it was. Perhaps, in your higher consciousness, you knew you were capable of more; knew that you could be more than a "good" person, that you could be a leader or an initiator. Perhaps you knew that you were capable of loving persons beyond your circle of family and friends—that you could open yourself to a universal expression of love and not limit yourself to a personal expression. Perhaps you were ready to move beyond simply being satisfied, to expressing joy, gratitude, praise, and thanksgiving.

In this particular example, creating a heart attack is like knocking down the boundaries of your heart center (your love center) and opening the door to the vastness of possibilities that lie ahead of you. By stopping yourself, you stop the limited activity of the past and take the rest time necessary to recoup, regroup, and begin again, anew, with the more of you you've discovered.

Whatever happened yesterday, *you* were involved in its happening. Reflect on it. What was wrong in your yesterday? Or, what was so right that you finished with it, and have done this radical thing to yourself in order to move on?

Speak to yourself now about then so that in the future you have a self with which to continue.

3

YOUR BODY: A FRIEND WHO IS TO YOU AS YOU ARE TO IT

Now that you have a clearer view of how you got where you are, let's *focus* on just where you are. Specifically, let's focus on where you are in your body, the vehicle through which you are living. Your body may not *yet* be involved in the dis-ease you are experiencing. Or, it may be preparing to manifest the effects of the dis-ease. Or, it may be suffering from the dis-ease. Indeed, it may be over-run with it by now. Whatever your stage of bodily involvement, it's important for you to be in conscious relationship with your body. In this sense, healing is as much preventative as it is restorative.

Remember earlier when we zeroed in on the fact that you and yourself are not one-and-the-same, but rather many-in-the-same one? And that your body was a part of the many, along with your feeling self, your rational mind and your Higher Self?

It's important to remember that again right now.

You are not your body! Your body is a *part* of you in that you are functioning through it on this plane of consciousness, but you are *not* your body. Neither are *you* your re-mind, your thoughts, or your feelings. *What* you are is larger than the sum of all your parts. In order to get on with the healing process, it's important that you communicate well with the various facets of your being and that the language you use in defining and verbalizing your condition is clear and accurate.

If your body has been crippled and you report, "*I* am crippled," you state an untruth. The truth is that your *body* is currently crippled. *You* are not crippled. If you say you *are,* you may well bring that into reality. You may cripple your ability to cope with your physical state; cripple your future by regarding it as permanently handicapped; cripple your relationships with others by seeing yourself as handicapped in relation to them.

Let's look at language clarification in relation to another facet of yourself. If your re-mind has tormented your little self into a state of paranoia and you say, "The world is out to get me; I need to protect myself from everyone," you take onto your total self the programming of your re-mind which is only *one* facet of yourself. Your re-mind thinks the world is out to get you. Your Higher Self knows that is not so. If you really tell it like it is, you should say, "My *re-mind* is in a state of paranoia." In this way *you* would remain detached enough to deal with the reality you have created for yourself.

There are so many examples. *You* are not being eaten alive by cancer, *the tissues* of a part *of your body* are what is being affected.

You are not unable to breathe, *your lungs* are struggling to draw in air.

You are not blind. It is only *your eyes* which cannot see.

You are not disfigured; your *appearance* has been altered.

Looking again at other facets of self, *you* are not unable to go on living because a loved one died. You are in the process of needing to bring new life and wholeness to *your little self* whose feelings were intertwined with another's, and to *your re-mind* which had constructed a pattern of two and requires new input so that you may reactivate the one (yourself) who was part of the two.

Or, *you* are not depressed. You are depressing *your energy* and building a hovel of grimness in which to dwell in desolation.

The form that you bring into being is the actual manifestation or result of your own initiation. Without going into all the formative steps in between, the process is the inception of an idea within your creative center and the flashing of that idea in actual shape on the screen of your world.

If you have a bodily condition, therefore, it is the direct result of your thoughts and your actions in combination with your environment, your genetic inheritance, and your particular human lineage.

I hope you really heard what I just said to you. We're back to the responsibility dimension to an important degree. It would be well to check out what you are choosing to think and feel right now. Whatever it is, be sure it's what you truly elect to bring into being. Whatever you thought or felt in the past will sooner or later be brought into being in some form in your body. You may become aware of the dis-ease while it is still manifest as thought or feeling, but if not, it may manifest itself in your body. Perhaps it already has. If so, you are in large part the cause of the effect you have produced.

If you chose to hear only what you had to say to yourself, what you agreed with, you perhaps silenced your outer ear's capability of functioning as a receiving set, in other words, created hearing deficiencies.

If you refused to let go of old thoughts and feelings, you might well have compressed your intestines and rendered them inexpressive, malfunctioning, in other words, prone to colon and bowel problems.

If you made your opinions rigid and unchangeable, you may have stiffened your joints and made them immovable, arthritic, rheumatic.

If you refused to see a wide range of possibilities in your life situation and limited yourself to a narrow view, you opened yourself to the limitation of your visual capacities, in other words, to eye trouble.

It is the *cause* that leads to the dis-ease of body, spirit, mind, or feelings, and *not* the effect. When finally the effect shows up in your body and you rush to a doctor, a chiropractor, a healer and yell HELP!, you are asking them to heal the *effect*—the visible result that you have labeled your ailment. While they may be able to do repair work on the effect, or even cure it, what is *wrong* remains. *The manifested effect is only the symptom of what's really going on.* Surgery may remedy the bone damage caused by arthritis, but only you can deal with the hard feelings that may have caused the calcium deposit to form, and which painfully affected the bone. The chiropractor may realign your spine, but you are the one who continues to go off the track in your life and to create disharmony. The psychic healer may move the energy and dissolve the effect, but you are the only one with control over how you utilize your energy and what you choose to reconfigurate.

Atomizers or pills may enable you to breathe more easily in the midst of an asthmatic attack. But, only you can open yourself to fully receive life as it offers itself to you through persons and events, rather than closing yourself off, choking yourself, gasping to overcome the block you may have set up to keep out the facet of life that seeks entrance.

The disharmony that appears as inability to breathe may well be little self struggling to deal with or express feelings.

To be cured in no way guarantees that you won't create the same condition all over again, or another one like it.

When you are in good health, it is partially be

cause you have created no blocks between your personality (your rational mind, little self, and body) and the source of conscious connection with your soul (Higher Self), and as a result your body has suffered no consequences.

Good health may also come as a result of your being in a state of abeyance in which little or no stimulation from one pole (one polarity of influence) to the other is occurring. However, at the same time little dramatic growth is occurring.

Whatever you do in your life is mirror-reflected for you in your body. Your body is shaped and formed by the vibrations you send out in actions and attitudes.

Your body does more than reflect for you, it is one of your best friends. As the old adage says, only your best friend will tell you the whole truth, holding nothing back. If you don't listen to your body when it talks to you, it takes direct action. It quits. It says, "No, I won't go."

Your re-mind will tell you what you should do, what you ought to do. Your little self tells you what you want, what you desire, what you feel. Your body has a far more direct way of communicating. It tells you what you can and can't do, and therefore, what you will and won't do. As long as you plan on using your body for whatever you're beginning to do, you'd be well to grant it full voting rights in the project.

Whenever you've gone too far, your body is the first to say so. It's a gauge through which you can measure the per-square-inch impact your vibrational self is having in your life.

When your body says "no" to you, what it is really saying is "yes." "No" to your plan of the moment; "yes" to your life in the future.

Right now, in your present state of crisis, you have much for which to thank your body. It may have registered alarm at your feelings and thoughts *before* getting ill, sending distress signals through headaches, shooting pains, exhaustion, severe tension or discomfort, even though you'd been able to find no physical cause for the symptoms. It may have bailed you out on your flight course just before you navigated yourself into a crash landing. Be grateful that you are alive to regret the state you're now in. You might not have had that privilege. It may have stopped you abruptly, but it didn't stop you *dead*.

Some of what I've said thus far may have been hard for you to swallow. In the long run it may be better medicine than some of those prescribed for your ingestion until now.

You could probably use some rest at this point. You've been working hard keeping up with me and I want to congratulate you—first for wanting to, and second, for doing it and sticking with it. If you can't see me, I want you to know that I'm smiling at you. I feel good about you. I've grown to feel very close to you. As a representative of my Higher Self, how could I feel otherwise? The Higher Self loves unconditionally. It receives rather than judges. As you explore further, practice receiving yourself. Offer any judgments of self back to their source, the re-mind.

Now rest.

4

YOUR PROBLEM IS AN OPPORTUNITY

If you are anything like most people, when you were first stricken your immediate thought was "Oh, no!" or "God, help me." You were more than stricken by the condition; you were *panic* stricken. You tried as hard as you could to make it not be so, to make it go away. When it wouldn't, you sank into despair. You may have even blamed it on your doctor. After all, the physician was the one who diagnosed it! Had it not been given a name, you might not be stricken with it.

You may have felt hurt and trapped. There seemed to be no way out, nowhere to go.

And if your friends and relatives were like most, they wept over you (or *for* you while they were *away* from you so that you wouldn't see, wouldn't be further upset). They soaked you in sympathy They, like you, could not understand how this could have happened to you. There was perhaps a sense in which the worse they felt in relation to you, the better you felt about *yourself*. Because you needed to *comfort them* in their discomfort about you, you had something constructive to do instead of just feeling sorry for yourself.

Maybe you're *still* experiencing the panic. Maybe you're still trapped, seeing no way out.

Like your relatives and friends, I, too, empathize with you. I can't feel your exact pain. That's yours. But I affirm that you have it, that you are the one suffering with it, not anyone else. When we get down to this fact, knowing what brought the dis-ease into being hardly seems to matter. The fact is that you're in the midst of it. What you want to know now is how to get out of it, how to move beyond it.

I want to participate with you in the process of bringing that healing into being. I'd like to give you a guarantee, but I have none. I'd like to do it *for* you. I can't.

I take that back. I *wouldn't* like to do it *for* you, even if I could. I'm not here to rescue you. Why, that would be tantamount to robbing you of your creativity, your ability, your opportunity.

I come to echo your own voice, not to take over your process or to live your life. I love you too much to attempt to rob you of that.

I'm not your salvation; you are. I wouldn't want you in any other hands. Yours are the sturdiest, the strongest, the most proficient you could have. I acknowledge the power I know is there.

I have a gift for you, my friend. It is the gift of looking at your current dis-ease in a totally new way. It is the gift of discovering that your problem is an *opportunity*. Your condition is a crown of new possibilities for you to wear, not a cross for you to bear. What I know to be true is that you have been blessed with the hope of profound life-change as a direct result of being abruptly stopped in your footsteps on an old path too-long trodden.

That's what a problem is. It stops you. It says you may not go on the way you have been going. It is a stone wall in front of you, one which seems, and often rightly so, insurmountable. A problem forces you to give up something, usually something very important. The greater the problem, the more you are asked to relinquish. The more you relinquish, the more space you create in which the new can emerge.

A problem is a powerful struggle between your little self desires and your Higher Self (or the God-self within you). When you say "NO" to what your inner divine wisdom asks of you, you have a problem. It is the "NO" that *is* the problem. When you say "YES," you have an opportunity. That "YES" *is* your opportunity.

I want so much for you to be able to hear this, to be able to say "YES," that you do indeed have an opportunity—even if you don't know what it is yet. That doesn't matter. Just to know that you *do have* an opportunity, lifts you out of the dense energy of the problem far enough to begin to see what the opportunities might be.

Can you see how exciting this is? I'm experiencing such joy right now. I joy in the knowledge that there is more than hope for you; there is new life, new possibility.

You have been stopped in order that you might start again, anew. The more serious your condition, the deeper your trouble, the more you needed to be stopped, the greater your opportunity. And you *can* handle it, even if you are feeling overwhelmed by it. If you were not capable of making a new shift, you would never have called a halt to the old. We are given (we give ourselves) new growth possibilities only when we are ready for them.

Of course, being ready and choosing to move on *in the readiness* with the new are two different things. In the first you tread water; in the second, you swim the lap. In the first you *talk* about it; in the second, you *do* it! I hope you choose the second. I hope you choose to move on. Self-pity gets to be a bore after a while. There's a lot of life in you and it's waiting to be lived.

In order to focus on opportunities, it is necessary for you to engage in some preparation so that you are ready to see what they might be. First, acknowledge that you *have* an opportunity (maybe yet to be discovered, but you *do* have one). Second, affirm that when you finally discover what the opportunity is, you may not *like* (little self) it, but it's yours nonetheless. In this way, you are ready for anything. When friends lament with you over your problem, that is a perfect chance for you to begin sharing with them the knowledge that this is more than a problem, it is also an opportunity, and/or precisely what you see to be the opportunities of your condition. By doing this, you are preparing to get on with the new rather than reiterating the old.

Another important preparation is to become friends with your problem. There's little point in viewing it as an enemy. If you do, you are at constant odds with it, in perpetual conflict. It makes healing all the harder.

Receive it as your friend, an energy configuration that's beside you constantly. It's closer to you now than almost anyone. You can talk to your dis-ease as a friend, negotiate with it, learn from it, even take leave of it. I invite you to come in from the battlefield and sit down at the peace table.

Once you've begun to perceive your condition as a possible friend, you will be ready to *ask it* to help you see its meaning. Just as if it were your buddy, you can confront it. You can speak to it. You can ask it, "What are you trying to tell me about myself?" You can open yourself to receive a reply.

Every condition, every dis-ease, has built into its very definition glimpses of what the opportunities might well be. Prepare for *your* opportunity by writing a definition of your condition, or what *you* say it is, and see what specific phrases are used to describe or talk about it. In those phrases lie the keys to the opportunities that await you.

I'll be of help to you as I can. It takes practice to be able to listen, detect, and pinpoint. I've had a lot of such practice.

If you are ready to get on with uncovering your opportunities, let us begin. Let us embark on a process which can open doors for you *no matter what your dis-ease happens to be*—a process that is a means toward healing because it enables you to discover that the problem is not something you have, nor something that has you. Rather, the problem is an opportunity you have given to yourself as a gift for your own soul growth. Having thus completed the preparatory steps, we are now ready to begin applying the process.

As we start, breathe deeply. This kind of exploration requires plenty of energy and fresh breath supply.

Put your problem across a table from you. Put it in its own chair. In this way, you see clearly that you are *not* your problem. It doesn't envelop the whole of you. You experience it in only certain facets of you. Now you can see it for what it is.

If you believe that there's strength in numbers, be reassured by the fact that there are two of us on your side of the table and only one over there. Even though that one has tried to gang up on you, we will not retaliate. We will remain in a state of harmony.

Since we're sitting at a table, how about putting some refreshment in front of you? Something tasty for your little self. Perceiving opportunities can awaken deep feelings, and little selves often need some kind of support during an exploration like this. You needn't make it something that will aggravate the dis-ease. If your problem is overweight, give your little self some frozen yogurt in place of an ice-cream sundae. (I know. I know. The other tastes better. But, would you like to know a secret? If your opportunity is to change your intake habits, you may find very quickly that once you begin to shift to healthier foods, your tastes will change and the sundae will be too sweet, even for you! "No way," you say. The question is, are you willing to try it? The problem lies in saying, "No way," in making no way possible. The opportunity is in saying, "Maybe," or "Let's see.")

Similarly, if you are struggling with alcohol, find something other than booze to put before your little self. Fresh-squeezed, ice-cold orange juice, for example.

Get something for your little self, some treat. And then, let's sit down together and talk with our friend across the table.

Are you ready? You're not afraid to look at your problem, are you? You invest your problem with power if you create fear in yourself in relation to it. You invest it with *your* power.

You're sitting at a peace table with your problem, not at an inquisition. You've come to find the joy, not to prolong the distress.

Did you just sigh? Good. Remember throughout to keep the breath flow going.

Since we're all starting out fresh with each other, I'd like to make a suggestion to you. Meet the problem as if for the first time. Rather than calling up all your past experience with it, all you *think* you know about it, all you've been told about it, all you feel about it, let it introduce itself, tell you its name, who it is, what it's like, what it does.

As it talks to you, listen to it as *a* problem, not as *your* problem. You two are separate from each other, yet related. You sit at the same table but not in the same seat.

The more cordial you are to it, the friendlier it is likely to be with you.

And remember, you are not alone. I'm here beside you—a mirror of your own Higher Self, able to see the whole, able to create harmony, able to handle anything.

Put pencil and paper before you. You might want to make some notes as we proceed.

Ask your problem what its name is. What does this condition call itself? Write it down.

Look into yourself for a moment. What's going on with you? How has the name of your problem affected you? Does it make you want to run for cover? Is it *that* terrible? After all, it is only a name. Remember what Shakespeare said, "What's in a name?" What's *in* a name is what you invest in it. There are some very loaded names in our civilized world, names like rape, cancer, mental illness, stroke, illegitimate pregnancy, TB. These names tend to be whispered. People shrink from them. "Don't let that happen to me!" Yet, the horror that is *in* the name is the horror we associate with it. The horror or fear is not inherent in the name itself.

No matter what the name conjures up, it is still only a name. To put your problem's name in its proper perspective, tell it what your name is. Well, go on, my dear one. Don't be shy. This is a process that could be very helpful. Have you told it *your* name? Good!

Now, ask it to describe itself. If it were a color, what would that color be? Ask it what its size and shape is.

(ASIDE: *I* know it's not there, just as *you* know. But it *is* there, isn't it? I know it may not have a color, or a size, or a shape. But then again, it might well have all three—either in your body or in your imagination. It *represents* something very real to you. That's why we're talking with it as if it were actually sitting in that very chair. The fact that it's not there is our little secret. The fact that it really *is* there can be our secret as well.)

Ask your problem what it does for (a) living. It works within you somewhere, is paid by you or lives off you in some way, or it wouldn't stick around. Ask. It will tell you.

Now reflect on yourself. What color are you? How do you experience your size and shape? What do *you* do to actively and consciously live? Tell your problem. Tell yourself. Write a description of you. Make sure your description is equally balanced. I'll be lovingly watching you. Everytime you write something that's not so great about yourself, put down something that's terrific. Don't cheat by short-changing yourself. Present your friend across the table with a balanced picture.

The more you like about yourself, the more you may find that is likable, or at least productive, about the dis-ease.

Ask your problem what it wants of you. Take time to let the answer come. Breathe deeply. Listen with your Higher Self. Close your eyes.

Ask yourself the same questions. What do you want of you? Again, wait for answers. Don't rethink an old thought. Allow the new to emerge for you.

Now, put it to your problem directly, as friend to friend. Ask it what opportunity it represents for you. What new can you bring into being in your life as a direct result of being stimulated by this problem? Take all the time you want with this. Be eager, open, joyful, ready. Let a multitude of possibilities enter your consciousness. *Want* to see the opportunities and you *will* see them. Let silly ones occur to you. Impossible ones. Get your inner tether ball swinging. Wrap yourself again and again around the pole of possibilities.

Go. I'll wait for you.

Perhaps even more will come to you as you engage with your own problem if you look at some examples. Let me do a few for you. The way *I* do it may not be exactly the way you are doing it. That's as it should be, for we each have our own creativity to draw on. The opportunities that come to me, may not be the ones that occur to you. That's fine. I can see only what *I* see, and you can see only what you see, for we see from different points of view. The specifics we arrive at are not nearly as important as the process in which we are engaging. The *process* moves the energy and sets healing in motion. The opportunities we uncover, though they too facilitate the healing, change and change again as we change. The more we utilize the process of seeking and finding, the more rapidly we change, and the opportunities we see shift and alter, too. *No one but you can tell you what your opportunities are.* By consciously engaging in the process of seeking them out, you will not only be able to begin to heal the current dis-ease you are dealing with, you'll be well equipped to engage with future dilemmas that life thrusts before you as new opportunities.

In the beginning, I told you this exploration would apply to any dis-ease you might be working with, be it spiritual, mental, physical, or emotional. What I'd like to do now is to give you some examples of the process of listening to a dis-ease by focusing on a sample from each of the four categories. I hope the samples will be helpful to you, and that they will spark you into even greater creative insight in relation to the specific condition you are dealing with in the general category.

I offer these samples in case you are saying, "Yes, I want to apply the process to my specific condition but I'm not quite sure how to go about it. Can you at least show me how you do it?" Or you may be saying, "I'll sit down and talk with the problem, but since I've never done this before, I have no idea what it might say or how it might say it. Can you let me hear how it speaks to you? Then I'll be more able to identify what is being said to me when I begin my own engagement."

It is in this vein that I share with you the following examples. May they be of service to you.

Across the table from me sits "Botched." That's the name of the problem in a shortened version. Its whole name is "Doing something stupid that botched an opportunity (again!)." The sound of the name makes me wince. Every time I botch an opportunity, I see myself as an idiot. I put botched in the general category known as mental dis-ease. Every time I botch something, my mind is critical of me. It sends me to stand in the corner until I fully understand how stupid I am.

The size and shape of this problem? Broken bits of fine china. A priceless cup and saucer smashed in a hundred pieces. I know that, although I am precious as fine china, I am in no way as fragile, as breakable. I am much more capable of surviving, of being able to be repaired from within, of being able to start again.

Though I know I'm capable of activating these qualities, I feel so terrible when I ruin a chance for myself that I actually forget that I *am* capable of surviving, of repairing, or starting again. Mostly, I imagine that I would botch it all over again, maybe even worse, if I were to try to make amends.

Botched lives off the remnants of hopes, dreams, plans and efforts which crumble around me because I bungle through life making a mess of everything. Botched gets to live longer in me because I judge myself a failure. Failures are flops at everything. I let my capabilities fall under my life table because I see myself as a loser. What else could I be when I always end up doing incredibly dumb things, or the consistently wrong thing at the consistently wrong time. Botched lives off me because I don't see myself as worthy of anything better or as capable of getting and keeping my life together in one piece.

When I see myself in this way, it's very hard for me to see any good qualities in myself. I feel they must be there, but I'm being so judgmental in relation to myself that it's almost impossible to climb up out of the prison of my re-mind and its brutal view of me, to see the good in me my Higher Self knows is there.

But then, maybe I did just climb out a little. After all, I *was* able to report my process, to see that I was stuck in my mind's judgment of me. I could do that only from the vantage point of Higher Self which is able to oversee the other facets of myself.

There may be hope for me yet, but probably not much. (There goes my mind again.)

Botched is like quicksand that pulls me in and buries me. It makes me want to scream for help. It drags me under.

As for a description of myself, it's really hard to say anything positive about myself when I'm so focused on what a loser I am . . . I can shift my focus. I can? Well, sure I can. This may sound silly, but shifting my focus comes in on me as a very novel idea in this moment. It means I have to put down my club and stop beating up on myself. That shouldn't be too hard. Who likes to beat up on oneself? Well, maybe I enjoy it a little. At least *I* can feel sorry for myself when no one else does and I am feeling deserted.

Shift of Focus From:	***To:***
I'm incredibly dumb	I do think of neat things, sometimes
I hurt the people I love most	I do know how to love deeply
I give the wrong things to the wrong people	I'm creative with my hands

Botched, what do you want of me? What do you want me to do? Botched tells me, "Let go of your image of yourself of always doing everything wrong. You actually bring botches into being by anticipating that they will happen. Simply do what you want to do with no expectation of how it's going to turn out."

What do *I* want? I want to stop being stupid. I want to stop hurting, to stop being hurt. I want to do everything perfectly, never make a mistake, never blow any situation again.

I just took a breath. Probably my first since I began. Rereading what I just wrote, I can see that my goals are somewhat unrealistic and that I set myself up for failure by demanding so much of myself. Right there I see my first opportunity. I can receive myself as I am without demanding that I be perfect. My Higher Self just said that I can take that a step further by receiving myself as I am *as* perfect. I don't think (there goes my mind again) I'm ready to go that far yet. I'm ready now to see what other opportunities there might be in this dis-ease for me. Okay, Botched, sock it to me.

Having just thought that, I can see that I'm already setting myself up to be knocked down by the opportunities, rather than helped by them. "Sock it to me," in its literal sense, implies my being hit with the opportunity. I now see that a second opportunity is to be more gentle with myself.

Botched, share with me what you see as opportunities that might help me out of the trap I've built for myself.

BOTCHED: What is it that you do that makes you think you are being like me?

ME: How long a list would you like? I say and do the wrong things most of the time. I give things to people who misinterpret my gifts. I say more than I'm asked to say and end up causing trouble. I talk myself out of jobs at the interview. I make advances, especially sexual, with what usually turns out to be the wrong person at the wrong time. Would you like me to go on? I've only just started.

BOTCHED: Are you sure that what you are describing is really doing something stupid?

ME: Of course!

BOTCHED: Who says so?

ME: Me!

BOTCHED: Perhaps an opportunity for you is to see that you are not a very fair judge of yourself. Maybe you are much harder on yourself than anyone else is. Maybe your greater "stupidity" (as you call it) lies in the fact that *you* label yourself stupid!

ME: That feels like a slap to the side of my head. Yet, I'm grateful for it. I'd rather have my stupidity reside there, than in actually being stupid. In a strange way, what you say is comforting.

BOTCHED: How do know you botched an opportunity?

ME: That's an easy one. In short, nothing happens as I would want it to!

BOTCHED: Right there is another opportunity. You are not God. Everything that happens does not depend on what you do or don't do. Everyone else who participates in a given event with you has a role in it.

ME: You mean it might be their fault and not mine?

BOTCHED: You are the one who mentions fault. I'm saying that you do what you do and that is all you can do. How others respond is up to them. You have no control over their response and therefore very little blame or even responsibility for it. However, bear in mind that it works the other way, too. If you say something and it evokes a good or positive response in others, you don't get the whole credit for that either because of the role they play in choosing and making a response.

ME: That's true.

BOTCHED: That's the cue to the next opportunity. You'd do well to start building a new self-image. People who feel good about themselves simply *choose* to. They don't see themselves as botching things. They see themselves as learning, growing, risking, finding their way. You do exactly what they do, only *you* call it stupid. Reshape your self-image by training your mind to label what you call your mistakes growth experiences rather than bloops.

ME: That will take work.

BOTCHED: One more thing. Laugh when you do something you think is stupid; joke about it. Tell your friends about it. If you let them laugh with you, you won't imagine they are laughing *at* you.

ME: Thank you.

BOTCHED: Don't mention it.

Perhaps now you have a better idea of the kind of engaging I was suggesting you do with your problem. The result of the process when I engage in it is that I have an active course of action to embark upon. By beginning to practice what I see as my opportunities, I set my healing energy in motion.

You may not want to invest energy in getting to know your problem any better. You may know it so well that you don't need or want any new input on that score. That's fine. If you know enough about the problem and yourself, then jump in with both feet and simply ask the problem to tell you what opportunities lie in it for you or ask your Higher Self to tell you and, *without censoring*, write down everything that comes. Censor later, if you must. It's fine to acknowledge that though something is presented as an opportunity, it is *not* an opportunity for *you at this time*. If you do that after you've recorded it, you'll at least be able to refer to it later, if you ever do perceive it as an opportunity in the future.

Let's move on to the area of physical dis-ease and take a brief look at what specific opportunities might make themselves known. An example is "Life-long dis-eases that do not kill you but hamper you," such as arthritis or back trouble.

In this sample and those that follow I'll speak to you *through* the dis-ease and point up possibilities that may or may not speak to you. It is appropriate that I speak *through* the dis-ease as Higher Self always speaks to us through our dis-eases (and through all our other life interactions).

> LIFE-LONG DIS-EASE: As a lingering dis-ease, I am ever present. In a sense, I am serving as a regulator for your life and how you live it. I was given to you as an on-going condition. I serve as a barometer or a check-point in your decision-making process. I cause you pain. I am sorry. That is the nature of my being. That is what I do.

Just because I'm on-going, you need not call me "life-long." By doing that you may be making a permanent place for me in your life. If instead you call me "as-long-as-needed," you open the way for me to finish and be out of your life.

Let's see if there is possibly a reason for my being in your life. Perhaps it's in my function, in what I do to you. I slow you down. I make you evaluate moves before you make them. I remind you of your fragility lest you push yourself beyond the point where you can comfortably sustain life.

An opportunity in being hampered is that you are being guided. To be constantly slowed down is to be alerted. To be pained is to be reminded; to be handicapped is to be tempered.

An opportunity here might be for you to move beyond the painful condition and find another way of being reminded and tempered. Perhaps listening more actively to Higher Self and less to "shoulds" or "oughts" (re-mind) is one such alternative.

As a chronic condition, I am often scorned, maligned, and medicated. Yet, might I not be seen as evidence of the God-force in residence in you?

Pleasure and pain are the polar ingredients of evolutionary growth. Ascending and descending waves of energy undulate in a dance of chemically positive and negative forces pausing for seconds in time to register upon the ether of the life-screen, the flash of being that says, "I am." Suffering and pleasure are two parts of the same whole, two halves of the same "I am."

The God-force resides in you. To *know* that is to know ecstasy. To experience that is to experience both pain and pleasure, for they are two sides of the coin of being alive.

Perhaps I am an opportunity for you to welcome me into the depths of your heart as the in-dwelling Lord. Shower me with love, be humble before my power and magnitude, be grateful that you are strong enough to know and survive the suffering I appear to cause in you. In your expression of unconditional love, suffering's polarity—pleasure—may make itself known to you in degree equal to your experience of suffering.

Back to back with pain, pleasure resides. If you could love me and cease fighting against me, we might become friends. Then we could exchange the gifts we have to give to each other and move on to new experiences. Perhaps this is your opportunity to move beyond complaining, to focus on *more* than the fact that you have limitations. Feel *more* than sorry for yourself, and maybe you will experience more than the one-sidedness of suffering. Express gratitude and praise loudly. Proclaim how blessed you are in the abilities you *do* have. Feel the wonder of the

God-force within you and perhaps you will encompass your suffering with ecstasy and become whole (that is, acknowledge that you *are* whole).

When you see that you are whole, you have the opportunity to move beyond the limitations you experience in order that you might see that in the final accounting *you* are the only real limiter of self. Your possibilities are in fact endless.

Chronic dis-ease may be the result of chronic holding back, which finally results in your actually being held back.

Describe me to yourself and see what possibilities await you.

Are you stiff in body?	Are your attitudes also unbending?
Do you limp?	Are you not standing on both feet and taking full charge of your life?
Are you stoop-shouldered?	Are you carrying more than your fair share of responsibility in a relationship?
Does your back trouble you?	Have you backed yourself into a corner? Or do you back down too often? Or do you get your back up over little things?

> Give yourself answers that allow you to move in new directions. This process is only the beginning. Please don't expect that a simplistic answer is going to remove the physical condition overnight. It takes a while to reorder the molecules of a manifested physical condition, especially a long-term condition. The answers you give yourself to questions such as these open doors to new beginnings.
>
> Gently begin new movement within yourself. Let it reflect in new movement in your physical body. The God-force is moving in you. Now let it shine out of you. Moving from the inside out may allow the sediment that restricts you to break up and fall away. Oil your machinery by loving yourself. I want you to be good as new as deeply as you wish it for yourself.

So, for now, ends the conversation with Lifelong Dis-ease.

If and when opportunities speak to you, the next step is to determine exactly how to make them a reality, to see what specific activities you might add to your daily life in order to make them real and substantive. That takes thought, concentrated energy, and application.

You asked what you could do. You asked, "Why me?" Once you show yourself, only you can bring the possibilities into reality. It's not as easy as taking a pill or an antibiotic, but it's far more creative. It asks a lot of you, while acknowledging that you have a lot to give!

I delight in being able to participate in the healing process. I can only hope that you do too.

Perhaps you've noticed that thus far, a key factor in pinpointing opportunities is *wanting to.* If you don't want to see them, you can be sure you won't. I've discovered this over and over again for myself.

If you say, "I *can't* see that," or, "I *can't* accept that," or, "I *can't* deal with that," you will *not* see, accept, or deal with that! To say, "I can't" is to close the door on the opportunity.

"I can't" is not true most of the time anyway. What you are really saying is, "I won't." "I *won't* see the opportunity," "I *won't* let go of the limited view I'm holding on to," "I *won't* move on to any other possibility."

There's nothing wrong with this, if that is where you want to be. If not, change "I can't" to "I am capable" (as a matter of fact, capable of almost anything) and "I won't" to "I will," and you will be most of the way home.

Under the category of Spiritual Dis-ease, let's explore the example of "Nowheresville" (lack of direction, dullness, stagnation, alienation).

If this is a time in your life when you find yourself in the middle of a symbolic lake and you are doing nothing more than treading water, you might be experiencing the painful dis-ease of being out of it, of belonging nowhere. You have no desire to swim to either shore of the lake. You don't necessarily want to drown. You don't know what you want to do, if anything, or where you want to go, if anywhere. You feel as if you could simply tread forever.

NOWHERESVILLE: Perhaps a main opportunity for you is to continue with what you are doing—nothing much of anything. Sometimes doing nothing is far righter for you than doing something which is forced, just for the sake of doing something.

If others are calling to you, making suggestions, trying to save you from yourself, encouraging you to get on with it, thank them and stay right where you are. They want to be helpful. They love you. But even more important, *they* are not in a treading period. They are doing and being *their* thing. Thus, from their perspective, it's time for you to be doing and being. It isn't satisfying to them for *you* to be doing nothing because it wouldn't be satisfying for *them* to be doing nothing. It's a natural reaction.

Simply acknowledge that what's right for them is not necessarily right for you. This is an incredible opportunity! It enables you to become your own leader rather than being dragged along by the rest of the group.

Keep your energy flowing. Keep yourself open to new possibilities. Keep yourself ready and alert so that when it *is* time for you to swim, you'll be in shape to make the necessary strokes.

I trust you are noticing that when the voice of Higher Self speaks—even through dis-ease—it gets right to the point. It is concise and sharp in its observations. If you find as you explore that the process is too objective for you in a given moment because you are hurting too much or are too subjectively involved, take a break. Get a snack. Call a friend. Reach out for an expression of love. Cry. Come back when *you* are ready. Only you know that. Honor yourself.

NOWHERESVILLE: Another opportunity in this condition is be alert to new possibilities that may be springing up in the oddest places. Have no expectations but rather abundant expectancy of what a new direction might be. When you remain free of expectations, you leave yourself open to possibilities. You say, in effect, "Something is out there for me, but I don't know *what* or *when* it will come into focus." Here's where abundant expectancy is so very important. You want to be ready when that "what," that special something, appears before you. You want to be alert to recognize it and ready to respond to it.

Living in abundant expectancy is like

> keeping your head above water while you tread rather than "going under" by bobbing up and down, sometimes seeing and sometimes not. It's keeping your senses sharpened so that you can quickly tune in the signal that begins to bleep in your inner receiving set, rather than risking missing it because you're busy broadcasting your alienation. It's looking out at the world through eyes that twinkle with joy rather than dullness. You *have* something to be joyful about—you've been granted the privilege of time in which to anticipate.

Once again, notice how opportunities present themselves with affirmativeness, with assertiveness. When you settle on what the opportunities may be for you in the dis-ease you're experiencing, you will want to fulfill them with the same affirmativeness and assertiveness. Then, your new life thrust will be exciting for you. I can hardly wait to see you set this energy in motion. You can be sure I'll be standing on the sidelines beaming with enthusiasm in my encouragement of you.

> If you are experiencing dullness, you haven't *yet* found that special something that turns you on. It's not that *life* is dull, it's that what you've done so far is perhaps dull.
>
> If you feel alienated, the feeling may be well justified. You have removed yourself

from the life flow. Naturally you now feel like an outsider. You *are* outside. Take advantage of your position. Look in. See what possibilities await you.

If you are stagnated, your record is stuck. It's playing the same groove again and again. There's something you haven't heard. You are allowing yourself to listen over and over until you catch it. Stay with your process. It's a good one.

Having no direction *is* having a direction. Going nowhere when you don't perceive where to go is going *some*where. The nowhere *becomes* the somewhere!

Stay true to yourself. Don't hurry. Let the future unfold for you. If you force it and find what you're *not* looking for, you'll have less than you have now.

When there is nothing, it is because something is waiting for you to recognize it.

So ends, for now, our exploration with "Nowheresville."

Let's do one more example, this time in the area of Emotional Dis-ease. We'll call this one "Loss of a Love." To me, a love relationship is very important. If it is to you as well, then losing it is like losing the whole world. Profound love is all encompassing. When it's gone, it seems as if *you* go with it. Looking for the opportunity in the loss is like an exercise in futility. Who *wants* new opportunities?

All you want is to have things as they were—to have your love returned to you.

Love is love, no matter what the relationship. If you are thirteen years old and he is fourteen and he touched your hand and you gave him yours, you have touched the same universal intensity that couples who have shared years together have known.

If you are sixteen and your teacher is twenty-five, a goddess or god, and untouchable; if you have yearned for her/him in your heart, loved her/him in your dreams, *you* know love.

If you are an adult and met your love in the few times possible, in secret hideaways, far from your established life patterns and obligations, if you burst in ecstasy in those scattered times, you have been in love.

If you've been married, united in a wholeness that only the two of you could have brought into being, you've been part of the power of love.

Having a personal love relationship is a serious business. I wouldn't blame you at all if, when someone told you, "You'll get over this loss," you wanted to bop the person over the head. No one knows how you feel except *you.* And yet, in the midst of the pain, there are opportunities for you, if you want to know of them.

LOSS OF A LOVE: First and foremost, if your partner is gone, what *you* had is not over. The love doesn't die, only the form of it changes. It is the same in nature. The seasons don't stop happening because one has ended. The cycle goes on. So does *your* love.

Leaves fall from trees and crumble. Your body aches as pain fills the gap left by your loved one. Suffer the ache. It's natural. It's good. Spring doesn't come until winter has fully expressed itself and taken its toll. Give yourself a winter. Take the time *you* need to hibernate and cry. Winters are different from each other. Some snow more than others. Some are colder. Let the loss of your love be as individual as was the *love* of your love.

Mourn your loss. Don't rush.

Here is your chance to love yourself *as* you loved the other.

Zip yourself up in the dark void of your inner being where it is warm and safe. Don't rush blindly (your eyes blurred by tears of loss) out into the world seeking replacement. There is no replacement. You will have lost both what you had and what you still have if you try to re-enact its specialness with someone else.

Be a friend to yourself in your loss. Care for yourself tenderly. Respect your need to pamper yourself and do it up round. Trust yourself to know your needs and provide others with the opportunity to give to you. (Not to inundate you, just to give to you in appropriate doses. Be your own physician. You prescribe what you need and when.)

As you mourn your loss, enjoy your gain —the gain of having loved. Enjoy the love that can never be lost. It's *yours* after all.

Breathe a lot, deeply. When you are ready, breathe in new life. Let the new life fill your environment. Get a flowering plant, a new painting, an ant colony. Put a potato in your closet. Let its growth and yours surprise you.

You've known a great love. You still know it. You still have your part of it to live. Here is an opportunity to continue to love the one who is gone by sending loving thoughts to him or her, by loving yourself, by smiling at people in the street, by loving others because *you know how.*

So ends, for now, the look at "Loss of a Love.'

These samples were meant to show you that there are indeed opportunities within every problem if you look for them.

The way to find out what yours are is to ask. As they come forth and make themselves known to you, receive and record them. When you are ready, and only you will know that, you can act on what you see the opportunities to be.

As you begin your personal investigation, you will find that the opportunities that present themselves are not generalizations that spring forth from the dis-ease as if for everyone. Rather, they are very specifically related to you because your interaction with the dis-ease and your reasons for having it are unique.

You may question your ability to find an opportunity in your current crisis because of how oppressive it is in your experience of it. If so, you might want to dip into your memory bank and find a time in your life, preferably several years ago, when you were in a crisis that was finally resolved. Ask your re-mind to call up the details for you, the despair you felt, the hopelessness. It may be similar to now. Remind yourself of how you got out of it. What did you do? Ask yourself now what your opportunities were *then*. The crisis today is no doubt entirely different. Yet, the fact that you survived before can encourage you to do the same now.

I support you in your search for your opportunities and encourage you to use the process outlined in this chapter often. As you explore, please know that more likely than not, you will find no quick cures for what ails you. The dis-ease which troubles you grew and developed over a long period of time and through much effort, even if unconscious. It was the result of a combination of many factors, not just one. It did not appear overnight. It began as a spark, a missed opportunity, which became enflamed. Now the dis-ease rages out of control and firefighters (counselors, doctors, nurses, friends) are frantically responding to the alarms you've set off. Even after the blaze is brought under control, smoldering ashes and charred remnants will need to be dealt with.

By moving now to seek your opportunities, you are once again igniting a spark. This time you are doing it consciously—not throwing an opportunity away as if it were a match stick, but using it to light a candle of new hope to show you the way to healing. The opportunity you find may not cure you instantly but it can bring you to a clearing in the midst of the fire and smoke, in order that you might get on with your life and move out in new directions.

5

AN APPROACH TO HEALING: CREATING THE NEW REALITY

Until now you've focused on where you were prior to being stricken, on how you got to where you are now, and on what opportunities await you in what's hurting you. From this point on, I'm proceeding on the premise that you *want* to actively involve yourself in healing, *want* to move on from your condition. It's just a premise. I don't make any assumptions about you, or about where you are. You helped give yourself the condition and may still need it. You may still be using your condition for healing what caused it in the first place.

If you aren't ready to fully move on, don't push yourself. It is fairly safe to say that if you move beyond a condition without having completely moved *through* it, it will either remain with you, or it will recur, perhaps to an even greater degree.

If you are *not* ready, don't go on with what I'm sharing. Stay with your own process.

If you *are* ready, let's get started.

As a first step, I'd like you to concentrate more totally on activating your Higher Self—especially its observer function. Remember, your Higher Self gives you an overview, enables you to see the whole picture. It shows you all that's going on while remaining detached from thoughts, feelings, and bodily sensations. Focus on monitoring the facets of yourself. Take, for example, your re-mind. What thoughts are you feeding yourself in relation to your condition? Is your re-mind scaring the life out of your little self by predicting doom, with jabs like:

You'll never make it through this.
You'll never be the same.
You won't be able to support your family.
You'll be crippled for life.
You won't be able to cope.

Thoughts like this run across your inner TV screen constantly, registering subliminally on your consciousness. They are by no means the only ones.

You'll be all right.
The medicine will help you.
You'll be able to adjust.
This can't last.
The healing will take time.

Both varieties, and others, move through in a steady stream.

As one or another variety predominates, an overall inner attitude toward healing begins to form. If you are not consciously aware of the thoughts you are registering, you eventually find yourself with a fixed attitude without knowing how it came into being. Then you say, "That's just how I feel about it" or, "That's what I *think* and that's all."

That last statement is more true than you may know. To say, "That's what I think" is to offer a view based on re-mind data stored in the computer bank of your previous experience. To add "that's all" speaks to the fact that you are closing out the knowing of your Higher Self, the feelings of your little self and the wisdom of your body and its manifestations. You have called *only* upon your re-mind and its thinking.

But if you are monitoring your re-mind with your Higher Self, you will not find yourself with an attitude that dominates your approach to the condition. You will instead be actively involved in the process through which an attitude comes into being. You will have something to say about it because you will be making choices in relation to the thoughts crossing your mental screen.

When your re-mind offers you the idea that you will never fully recover, you, from the vantage point of your Higher Self, can actively engage with your re-mind in a number of ways. You can tell it, "That's what you think." You might pursue this by pointedly asking, "On what basis do you make that statement? What data do you have to support that?"

Then let your re-mind respond to you. Insist that it be accountable to you, and engage with it until you are satisfied with the exploration.

If you've never consciously done this before and you feel a little awkward about the possibility, let me give you a little sample. It doesn't embarrass me to do it, or to have you eavesdrop on my process. The important things for you to hold in your consciousness are (1) that the Higher Self always concentrates on the here-and-now, and (2) the Higher Self knows. In contrast, the re-mind does not know, it merely thinks (and paradoxically, it thinks it knows.) Secondly, the re-mind brings up thoughts, suppositions, assumptions, expectations and predictions—all patterned in the past and related to the future. That's how you can tell the difference between your Higher Self and your re-mind. It's not that one is better than the other; it is that each serves its own particular function.

RE-MIND: You will never fully recover.

HIGHER SELF: That's an incredible thing to say.

RE-MIND: Why? (Re-minds enjoy asking why questions even though they are seldom, if ever, helpful.)

HIGHER SELF: (Ignoring the "why" question) The incredible thing about that statement is the use of the word "never." You are perhaps able to tell me what my state is right now. You have no way of knowing what the future holds.

RE-MIND: The odds are that you will not recover fully.

HIGHER SELF: I am not a statistic. I am a unique individual with my own particular capacities for healing.

RE-MIND: Yes, but (a favorite re-mind rebuttle and static-causer) your chances are slim.

HIGHER SELF: Healing is not a matter of chance.

RE-MIND: (It might come up with a variety of jabs here, depending on the particular condition.) It runs in your family; (or) Most people don't recover from this; (or) You're not strong enough to cope; (or) Even the doctors don't know a cure; (or) The damage has already been done.

HIGHER SELF: All of what you've said contains elements of truth. But elements are not the whole picture. You cannot splinter the wholeness of the truth that I know by shooting fragments of fact at me.

Or, taking another approach to the same monitoring process:

RE-MIND: You're going to make a full recovery.

HIGHER SELF: How do you know that?

RE-MIND: I believe you will.

HIGHER SELF: Belief is not a very reliable approach.

RE-MIND: Well, what about the power of positive thinking? (Re-minds often carry their own cheering sections.)

HIGHER SELF: It is true that to think positively is to create an environment in which healing *may* be speeded up, in which I *might* fully recover.

RE-MIND: I don't see any difference between what I said and what you said.

HIGHER SELF: "Will" and "might" are two entirely different words. There are no definites, no guarantees. You think I can impose my desires on my situation. I *know* that I contribute to my situation significantly, to be sure; but that is far different from the imposition of desire.

RE-MIND: If you do all the right things you should (another favorite re-mind word) get the results you want.

HIGHER SELF: I do what I know to do in each new moment. What I do is neither right nor wrong. As to results, I choose to proceed with no expectations so as to refrain from building in the possibility of disappointment. Furthermore, what I *want* (little self's word for identifying its desires and wishes) may not be what is ultimately harmonious for me.

RE-MIND: I don't understand you. (Making sense of things IS a re-mind function.) Don't you want to get well?

HIGHER-SELF: I am concerned with learning from my condition and participating in the healing process. That may include "getting well" as I, from your point of view, might define it; it may not.

It's the monitoring process I'm concerned with now. You'll be getting pertinent signals from your little self and body as well. If you are in touch with the needs of your little self, they will not become all-encompassing. They will not drain your energy or draw you away from your overall focus on healing.

Your little self needs to be cared for by you—mothered and fathered by you.

When your little self says, "I am frightened," wrap your arms around him or her, and speak gently.

HIGHER SELF: I know you are frightened. You don't have any way of knowing what might happen next. You don't know what to do. You worry when you are in the dark.

LITTLE SELF: I feel so lost and helpless, so inadequate.

HIGHER SELF: You give me a great gift when you express your feelings. You experience helplessness because there is nothing *you* can do about our present circumstances. I *can* do something. I can move ahead with the healing process. When *you* make me aware of the feeling of helplessness, I am sparked into immediate action, into helping myself. If you weren't feeling, I would not be made aware of what was going on in us.

LITTLE SELF: You make it sound as if I'm doing something important while I'm simultaneously feeling inadequate.

HIGHER SELF: Indeed you are.

LITTLE SELF: You encourage me to share another feeling.

HIGHER SELF: What is it, dear one?

LITTLE SELF: I don't like being in this condition. I'm hurting.

HIGHER SELF: That too is important for me to acknowledge. A part of getting on with healing is the comforting of the self that is hurting. From your vantage point you experience us to *be* in this condition. That could hurt a great deal. Perhaps it will be of some comfort to you to know that we are neither *in* the condition nor *of* the condition. We are moving *through* the energy of the condition as a ship moves through a storm at high sea. Our vessel is thrown about mercilessly. We struggle to survive. But storms do not last forever. They are an indication of a disturbance in our environment. When the forces are brought into harmony, the storm passes, having run its course.

LITTLE SELF: Will you be beside me while it's storming?

HIGHER SELF: I will be beside you always.

Using metaphors and analogies, like comparing the condition to a storm, is very helpful in carrying on Higher Self and little self communication. Little selves always enjoy stories and parables. When great spiritual leaders teach in parables they are touching the larger populace with wisdom in the form that is easiest to receive. It is a loving way for a spiritual elder to share with a novice.

As with your re-mind and little self, so your body will be very straight with you in terms of its needs, if you are willing to listen. It will nix or encourage certain foods and exercise patterns, among other things.

PHYSICAL BODY: Fine state of affairs I'm in! Nobody listens to me. I warned you this would happen. Now look at what you've done.

HIGHER SELF: I acknowledge you as being very wise. You were deserted, left to flounder on your own. You were not listened to. You did well to manifest the deficiencies in a form so that they could be seen, so that they *had* to be dealt with.

PHYSICAL BODY: I'm glad you are willing to acknowledge that. What I did was to quit. My murder was being planned and I had no intention of being passive to the point of being a corpse. I spoke up out of desperation. Where were you during this time?

HIGHER SELF: I was here. I was aware of what was going on. I was not called upon. I was not activated in order that new choices might be made. Thoughts and feelings replaced me. All that I could do in the meantime was carry out my function as observer and wait.

PHYSICAL BODY: *You* may be able to wait, but not me. I end up battered and bruised.

HIGHER SELF: That is because you are energy-in-form. You did the only thing you could. You brought into manifestation what was going on.

PHYSICAL BODY: Thanks for the stamp of approval. It's more than I've gotten up to now. Everyone has been jumping all over *me* for being sick and nobody seems to mention that this was done *to* me because it was demanded of me by actions taken or not taken. Believe me, it's not easy to be a body in this world. If anyone has the right to ask, "Why me?"—it's me.

HIGHER SELF: Perhaps now that you've made your point more clearly than ever before, more attention will be focused in my direction. New choices will be made. Healing will proceed. You will be able to bring a new form into being.

Once you take charge and actively engage with the facets of yourself as we've just done, you can begin to bring into being new realities which will not only bring you healing but joy. If you are alert and ready to tune into your Higher Self, I'd like to introduce you to a way of actually bringing that new reality into being.

A reality is whatever is real to you. Other persons might have what would appear to be your exact condition, yet their perception of the condition may be totally different from yours—they have created a completely different reality about it. You might view it as an affliction, for example, while for another it might be just another problem to live with.

The reality you create can be changed at a moment's notice. Instant faith healings may well occur in this way. The suffering go to a healer or to a site like Lourdes, stricken with a reality they've locked themselves into. There they open themselves more totally than ever before to a completely new possibility, and become the new or create the new that they see in a flash of light which they later refer to as an act of God or a miracle.

A simple shift toward creating a new reality is to move away from concentration on the fact that you are down and incapacitated. Once having registered the fact that you are, you can refrain from investing any further energy in it. In this way you do not hold yourself in a blocked position. You simply acknowledge a reality, reminding yourself that it is only *one* of many possible realities.

You can begin consciously to create a new reality by concentrating your attention on the energy that is constantly moving through you, and beginning to activate and direct it. Let's do a few warm-ups. As you read through each of the following sections, follow the instructions as you go along.

Activating Your Energy

Rub the palms of your open hands and your fingers together quickly and vigorously. This is a very simple way of stirring up energy. Now, place your hands together so that your palms and fingertips are touching. With your eyes closed, breathe in deeply through your nose and create the awareness of a circle of energy beginning at your point of inhalation and traveling through your right shoulder and arm, through your right hand *to* your left hand, up your left arm and shoulder and back to the point of origin. Repeat this several times.

Continue to breathe deeply in the circle of energy and separate your palms slightly while keeping your fingertips together. Note whether you can feel the energy traveling in the space between your hands. You might feel a tingle, a flow of warmth, a stream of movement. If you feel nothing, simply continue without being concerned. You feel nothing, yet. Leave it at that. For some people, this takes a lot of practice. If you need to practice, do so.

Now separate your fingertips as well as your palms a little, and open yourself to the energy circling in the space between your hands. Be sure to continue to breathe deeply.

Begin to move your hands slowly, rotating them near to each other in order to sense the differing waves of energy. See how far apart you can pull your hands and still feel the energy.

Let your hands rest. You may find that they are puffy. This often happens when we focus on sending energy through a specific part of the body.

You might want to try this experience with a friend by putting both your hands together with your friend's (palms to palms, fingertips to fingertips) and following the same course of action. Then compare your experiences. Becoming aware that you receive, send, transmit—that indeed you *are* energy —is a key step in activating healing energy in you.

Utilizing Energy on Self and Others

Breathe deeply, activate the energy in your hands by rubbing them together, close your eyes, and slowly bring your hands toward your face and head, palms facing you.

See if you can sense your hands near your face before they actually arrive there.

Continuing to breathe deeply, slowly and gently move your hands around the area of your face and head, close to, but not actually touching, your skin. Feel the movement of the energy in the area.

Try sweeping gestures so as to experience larger movements of energy. This is especially helpful when you have a headache and want to move the energy. You can begin at the base of the neck and sweep up and out, always staying close to the surface of the skin but not actually touching it. Beginning high above the head, sweeping down and in and moving the energy as though your hand were a magnet pulling it toward your head and through it, is a way of bringing energy in when you are feeling depleted or low. Remember that your hand follows the contour of the head without touching it, for you are interacting through the energy itself, not the physical form of it. Try this with a friend and see if you feel as much energy from your friend's hand as from your own or vice versa.

After you and your friend practice a little you might want to give each other full-energy body massages. This can be done fully clothed except that it is advisable to remove shoes with leather soles. Have the person lie on the stomach first and then on the back. Holding your hands several inches above the physical body, let your hands move freely in swirls, or in straight paths as if you were pulling taffy with your palms, or up and down. Do what feels good to you. Proceed intuitively. Everyone has healing hands —hands through which energy travels. People who say they are healers simply acknowledge that they are, and practice their skills. They allow the fullness of their love to flow while the receiver heals himself or herself by allowing his or her own energy to flow out of the area of congestion and into the free-flow of the life-force.

Open yourself to be a channel of energy and let it pour through your hands. Cup your hands so that the energy is directed through the center of your palms rather than being diffused and rushing off the sides of your open hands. Scan the body for hot and cold spots. They may correspond to where the subject is feeling pain or tightness.

A hot area might have an over-intensity of energy. You can contact it and move it by rotating your hands in that area, by starting close to it and moving down and out toward the extremities, or by starting close and moving straight up, slowly. Repeat these movements as often as it feels good.

As you do this to your friend or to yourself, focus only on being a channel of energy. You are not a doctor. You are not doing anything *to* this person. You are providing your friend (or yourself) with the opportunity to move his or her *own* energy. Don't focus on what *you* want to see happen in this person. Focus only on the larger pattern of harmony coming into being.

Be sure not to ignore the soles of the feet. The road map of the entire body is imprinted there with parts of the foot corresponding to organs in the body. Sometimes you can help to facilitate the flow of energy through the entire body by simply holding your open-faced hands a few inches from the soles of the feet. You can feel the flow coming from the feet and through your hands, and vice versa.

Sharing in this way with a friend is a way of setting your own healing energy in motion. By sending energy *out* through you, you invite fresh energy in.

You may be wondering, "Can this actually help me?" If you are open to it and you trust that it can, it can and will. I use it all the time. I once wrote thousands of labels over a two-week period. Then my thumb gave out. It quit. It cramped up and was unusable. I used my other hand to give it an energy massage. After about fifteen minutes the pain began to ease. After a few hours of periodic massaging, it was well and ready to go again.

On other occasions I've banged a part of my body with a force that usually leads to a large black and blue mark and/or swelling. But by *focusing* on the site in the moment of its happening, *knowing* that there is no need for disharmony to register there, *moving* the energy until I feel the sting dissipate under my energy touch, I have had no swelling, no mark, but rather, instantaneous healing. I have done the same with bleeding. By focusing the energy I have coagulated the blood immediately.

Instantaneous healing occurs in the consciousness. When persons are unaware that they can exercise this power of consciousness, they subjugate themselves to their bodies and let the body work it out. The body does work it out—but from the depth of the wound to the surface—and it simply takes a lot longer.

By being more aware of your own energy rhythm, by breathing deeply and being open, by participating more actively in creating your own reality, consciously, you open yourself to the gift of self-healing.

Moving Energy on the Breath-Flow

Let me guide you on a journey into yourself. Come along with me at your own pace. Do a sentence at a time, or a phrase at a time. Do each fully, closing your eyes and deeply experiencing it before moving on. Take as much time as you need and want during each pause. Perhaps you could have someone else read this to you, pausing appropriately (or where suggested) so that you could focus totally on the journey itself and not have to be interrupted with reading the words. Be sure to choose someone whom you trust, someone whose Higher Self is clearly functioning. You might even want to tape your own voice so that you can guide yourself through the process. If you have chosen a route other than reading this to yourself, close your eyes during the entire experience.

Inhale slowly through your nose. Draw the air in deliberately, purposefully. (*Pause.*) Listen to the sound the air makes as it passes through your nostrils. (*Pause.*) Fill the whole of the inside of your head and exhale equally as slowly. (*Pause.*) Pull the air down through your neck into your chest, down further to your diaphragm, an elastic muscle beneath your rib cage. Feel your midsection expanding and contracting. (*Pause.*) Experience the lulling effect on your body. (*Pause.*) Inhale and exhale to a drawn-out count of three—three to bring it in and savor it, three to release it with ease and love. (*Pause.*)

Imagine the air surrounding you in a soothing color—one that speaks to you of healing. (*Pause.*) See the colored air whirling gently about your face, softly caressing your arms, your hands. (*Pause.*) Breathe the air in and fill the inside of your head with color. Then let it emerge through your eyelids. (*Pause.*) Breathe it in again, enveloping the inside of your chest cavity with soothing color. (*Pause.*)

Draw it into your arms, your legs; release it through your fingertips and toes and let your entire body be held afloat in a fluffy cloud of healing hue. (*Pause.*)

Begin to sense the texture and density of the air you are drawing in. Compare it with the texture of your physical being as you bring it in. (*Pause.*)

See where in your body you are manifesting this condition of dis-ease. Where are you trapping or congesting? (*Pause.*)

Establish a clear line between the entry point of the air into your body and the congested area of your body. (*Pause.*)

Breathe the air into you and along that line or pathway. Breathe it deeply into the area of pain or congestion. (*Pause.*)

See the color of the congestion, the shape it takes. (*Pause.*) Go deep into the shape and color of the congestion. See it as the same size as you. Feel it throughout your whole body. (*Pause.*) See it as a separate entity. What does it look like? What is it threatening to do to you? How is it trying to hurt you? (*Long pause.*) Imagine what would happen if it took over your whole body. See what you would look like, what state you would be in. (*Pause.*)

Go deeply into your fear, your outrage. (*Pause.*) Cry if you need to cry, wash this dis-ease away with the purity of your tears. Go deeply into the pain and become one with it. (*Long pause.*)

Slowly lift yourself out of the dis-ease, the pain, the disharmony. (*Pause.*) Raise the essential you of you just enough above the dis-ease so that you are detached from it and can see it. Rest there, breathing deeply. Do not engage with the dis-ease any more. See it as if it were frozen in time. (*Pause.*)

Now move still another step beyond the dis-ease and beyond yourself. Move into the void, the cosmic void in which there is no sickness, no tension, no fear, no emotion—the cosmic void in which there is only knowing. Be there in the nothingness, in the detachment. (*Long pause.*)

Experience within yourself the reordering of your inner molecular structure. Restructure and reorder the molecules of the dis-ease. Break up the pattern of dis-ease. Let go of old ways of thinking about it and reacting to it. (*Pause.*) Move into a state of total openness, total newness. (*Pause.*) If the condition began in relation to another person, forgive that person. To forgive is to release energy you have been holding back from another and to use it for giving to that person. (*Pause.*) Forgive yourself for participating in the creation of this dis-ease. Forgive yourself; give love energy to yourself. (*Pause.*) Receive yourself as beautiful exactly as you are. (*Long pause.*)

As you exhale, breathe out the adhesive energy with which you held the congestion together. (*Pause.*) Breathe in release and freedom. (*Pause.*)

Let go in unconditional surrender. Let go of the condition. Let go of any conditions you have placed on yourself and on your life. (*Long pause.*)

Slowly, in your inner self, begin to create harmony in your own being. Using the energy of the dis-ease, create a new shape for it, become friends with it, become one with it. Become whole; heal yourself. (*Long pause.*)

Take the time to absorb what you have just got in touch with. What new possibilities have you opened up for yourself? What would you like to pursue further? Share some of your insights with others; it's a good way of reinforcing them. Utilize this approach as often as you wish. You will constantly uncover new facets to deal with as you activate your healing energy on the breath-flow.

There are two other important things to remember when you focus on reality creation. Refrain from speaking about the stricken state as *your* illness, *your* condition, and you won't be locked into owning it as *yours*. Second, remember that it is no accident that you are in your present circumstances. There is a purpose and design to everything in life, by no means fatalistic, but by all means significant and meaningful. Your healing will be no accident either. You are playing a significant and meaningful role in it.

6

THE VOID–AND OPEN-ENDED PRAYER

Begin with a deep breath. Now do it again, and when you inhale, ask yourself, "Who am I?" When you exhale, answer, "I am . . ." and fill in the blank spontaneously. "I am me." "I am weary." "I am reaching." "I am ready." "I am never going to make it." "I am getting stronger."

Make this little exercise a part of every day. Do it when you wake up, at odd times during the day, and before going to sleep. Always begin with the deep breath so that you clear the channels. As you do the exercise, consciously note that each time you answer, you come up with another response. The answer is different each time because you are different each time you ask the question.

Monitor the kinds of answers you give yourself. Are they valid? Valid responses state truth, yet in no way do they invalidate the self. If you ask, "Who am I?" and the answer is, "I'm a loser," that is an example of one that is invalid. The truth is *you are a person* who has lost out in certain specific wants and desires. The two are very different.

Practice affirming yourself by speaking truth and you will not invalidate yourself. Or to put it another way, you will not make an invalid of yourself.

By recognizing that you are new in each moment and with each fresh breath, you remove yourself from being locked into past views of yourself and of your condition. You activate healing energy.

Some other questions you might want to practice asking with the breath are, "How am I?" or, "What am I feeling?" or, "Where am I with my condition right now?"

Breathing, asking and answering from a fully here-and-now focus facilitates the creation of your new reality. It keeps you up-to-date with who you *are* rather than with who you *were* when the dis-ease struck.

When you have explored, dealt with, received, and moved on completely from association with the past, when you have acknowledged the facts, the opportunities, as they exist in the present, then and only then are you ready to ponder, "Where do I go from here?" That question opens a very special door.

The door leads to the void. The most significant quality of the void is that there is nothing there—nothing to see, touch, or feel. Nothing to grasp hold of, nothing to bank on, or feel secure in. The void is just what its name implies.

The void is a space of nothingness. It is pure blackness, radiant with light. It is formless—neither hopeless nor hopeful. The void is the workshop in which harmony is produced. It is the space which may be entered by the worker-on-self who is ready to know the larger meaning of the dis-ease in his or her life. It is for the worker-on-self who is ready to give up the condition. Translated in the void this means giving up the conditional response to life that led to the dis-ease in the first place.

When you have a conditional response, you are in effect saying, "I'll do this *if* you do this," or, "I'll do this *but* you must do this," or, "I'll do this because I want this to happen."

When making such deals it is important that both sides agree to the terms. If you are making a contract with another person, it is fairly easy. However, when you make such an agreement with life itself, you have no deal, even though you say you do. Life is not an objective contractee such as another person might be. Life is a process in which nothing is stagnant or true to form. Life is inconstant, ever-changing, unpredictable, larger than any individual self who lives it.

Let's check out what kind of deals you might have made with life, or rather, what kind of terms you might have imposed that led you to your current condition.

Did you say to life, "I'm going to bottle up my feelings because I know that others can't take it when I express them"? As a result, have you created a condition of inner drowning?

To move beyond the condition, you must let go of your conditional responses to your feelings, to release them unconditionally, and to allow others the right to deal with their own feelings in response to yours. Life gives you only your *own* life to live. It does not invite you to live the lives of others. If you are trying to live theirs, who is living yours in the meantime?

Did you say to life, "I'm going on with driving my body to match my ambition, and if my body doesn't want to it's just going to have to shape up to meet my desires"? Was the resultant condition a stroke, a pure tit-for-tat blow to mirror for you how you were mercilessly striking your body with the whip of insatiable wishes?

To move beyond, release your dictatorial demands and move into a partnership of equality with your body. Life gives you one physical body. You can place whatever demands you want on it. Life also demands that you reap the harvest of what you have sown. You cannot speak for yourself *and* your body. It has its own voice.

Or, did you say to life, "I will totally devote myself to my husband and in this way he'll remain faithful to me. I'll do everything for him. I'll meet his every need. I'll be everything he could ever want in another person. He won't be able to do without me. He'll be dependent on me"? Events don't necessarily work out in a particular way simply because you act in a given fashion. Oftentimes it is for the very reason that another feels dependent on you that he or she runs, seeking freedom—seeking to be his or her own person.

It happens in so many kinds of relationships. There are parents who rush in to handle everything for their children, even to the point of convincing them that they know what college and what profession is best for them. When children are young and growing, they want to depend upon their parents. It's part of the loving and nurturing process. But as children grow into an awareness of themselves, they want to express their individuality. Parents who sacrifice *for* their children, sacrifice their *children,* for they tend never to let them forget what was done for them. When the children feel the overzealous love trap and try to escape, their parents lament, "Why us?"

Is your current dis-ease a result of your having devoted yourself to another and then been abandoned, or cheated on, or widowed, or rejected? Did you feel that the person did it to you on purpose? And did that feeling grow out of the conditional overlay you created in the first place? You are the one who decided to devote yourself and you are the one who decided (had expectations about) what would come into being as a result. You got zapped because none of us has the power to determine what the results will be. You were hit because you *thought* you had the power. You are in a state of dis-ease because of your conditional interaction with life.

If this is indeed what you did, I hope that you are glad to have the insight now to see it. I haven't mentioned all this to put you down. To the contrary, it's not that you did something wrong but rather that it is important for you to know the properties of conditional responses. By knowing what they are and what havoc they can produce, you are in a better position to make a choice about whether or not you want to create a conditional response and thus open yourself to the possible consequences. Sometimes a slight tempering of a conditional response can make all the difference. For example, you can reason *if this, then this* as long as you add a *maybe.*

Maybe takes us one step deeper into the void. What is revealed there is *Have no expectations but rather abundant expectancy.*

An expectation is a fixed view of how something will happen or what someone else will say or do. By virtue of its very construction as a word, an expectation leaves little room for the unexpected. If you have an expectation and it goes unfulfilled, you are disappointed, resentful, unhappy, let down. You seek something or someone on whom to place blame.

If you are looking for someone to blame, there is always yourself. You are the one who set up the expectation. You disappointed yourself by limiting the outcome before it ever had an opportunity to take shape. Of course, you needn't invest *any* energy in blame at all—no blame of yourself, or of the other person, or of life. You can be a lot easier on all three by simply acknowledging that you had an expectation and it didn't work out the way you thought it would. Blame has nothing to do with it. You did what you did, period. Now you can create a new reality and do something else.

Throughout, you can simply love yourself, regardless of what you did or what you will now do.

While expectations can be a source of complication, expectancy is quite a different energy interaction with life. You know that something is going to happen. You simply don't know what. You stay open and expectant without predetermining how something will turn out. Instead you allow yourself to be surprised by what does.

Living in expectancy is active, not passive. You are still free to plan, to hope, to wish, to channel your energy in a particular direction, toward a particular end.

However, you do not lock yourself into those plans, hopes, and wishes. You see that there are possibilities beyond the ones you envision in a given moment. You leave yourself open, with healing life energy flowing unblocked, not locked in by expectations.

In relation to your dis-ease, if you have expectations about exactly how the healing process will take place and what the result will be, you might be setting yourself up for a dangerous fall. If the healing doesn't proceed accordingly, you might think that no healing is taking place, while in fact, a form of healing unknown to you might be in process. If you reject the form because you have limited yourself to some other configuration, you might well be denying your own healing out of pure lack of recognition.

If your expectation is that when this is "over" you will return to your state of living as it was before you were stricken, you may either be very disappointed by the fact that your expectation does not materialize, *or* you may be even more disappointed that it does! Your dis-ease may have caused such a profound shift in your energy body, that to return to your former state is a journey into the lesser, because you are now ready for the more.

Prayer is a very powerful means of bringing energy into focus. It is a way of calling the initiating force of the universe into action for a specific. Paradoxically, prayer offers both hope and temptation. The hope is that your prayer will be answered. The temptation is to pray with that expectation. If the prayer is met, then "God is good." If not, what then?

God *is* good. Good is not defined in terms of getting what you determine *you want*. Hence, when you pray for good to come to you, you are praying for God to become manifest in you, for God's will to be done. When you pray, "Thy will be done," you are praying a prayer of expectancy. That is very different from the prayer of expectation. "God's will" is *always* being done. It is done *consciously by you* when you acknowledge it, receive it, express willingness to move on with it and through it rather than fighting it or attempting to make it disappear.

It is done consciously by you when you engage in open-ended prayer. Open-ended prayer is the acknowledgment that you don't know everything; that you may not yet see the larger purpose in your dis-ease. You may have preferences as to your recovery and you are actively requesting them, but you affirm that you are merely making a request and that you are open to what the universe has in store for you in the unfolding process of life. Open-ended prayer is praying for the manifestation in you of what is harmonious for you, of what is contributory to your soul growth. In open-ended prayer you are not placing yourself in the hands of something called Fate. Rather, you are opening yourself to the highest and best that can come to you and to the highest and best you can be. This has much more to do with how you *respond* to what does result than with the result itself.

You activate your energy and begin to create a new reality by adding the dimension of praise and thanksgiving to your prayers. This is the healing process you consciously engage in while you dwell in the interim called the void, while you wait for the answers to your prayers to become clear. You relinquish struggle, nay-saying, fighting against. You give up feeling sorry for yourself. You refrain from worry. You consciously focus on what is and offer thanks. You activate healing by being grateful for all things, by directing love energy to the dis-ease that resides in you.

"Thank you, heart, for shrieking so loudly at me that I might become cognizant of how I was attacking you. Thank you for the opportunity to seek a new life style and to be easier and gentler with you and myself."

"Thank you, loved one, for dying when it was in harmony for you to go. Thank you for years of such deep living that I now weep in heavy grief over the loss of you. I would not experience such loss had I not been blessed with your profound love to begin with."

"Thank you, eyes, for refusing to see, since I have refused to see. Thank you for enabling me to turn inward and awaken capacities I never knew I had—to perceive, to absorb, to assimilate, and to bring into new form."

"Thank you, world, for leaving me abandoned to my desperate loneliness in order that I might see that only *I* can fulfill my needs for wholeness."

"Thank you, cancer, for causing me such excruciating pain as you eat away at my tissues that I might be in touch with the greater unfelt pain that I caused my soul as I ate away at the fabric of my spirit."

"Thank you, thief, for robbing me of my possessions in order that I might see things in their proper perspective."

"Thank you, God, for the slaying of my son in war, for now I see how the taking of sides ravages the wholeness of truth. The sons of the enemy die equally. That equality was the oneness we tore asunder by dividing ourselves on issues and offering ourselves, the divinity of our spirits, as sacrifices to ideas of the mind, to matters of opinion to which we gave the label 'holy.' "

"Thank you, leg, for breaking beneath me, for showing me the imbalance of my step, the twistedness of the pathway I had paved for myself."

How can you say such thank yous? You find it difficult, you say, to praise what you refuse to accept? There is your answer. First say, "yes," to yourself and to your dis-ease. Then ask yourself if you *want* to say, "thank you," if you want to receive your problem as an opportunity. If you don't want to, you will not be able to! If you don't want to, forget it. There is no way, there is no *how,* without first wanting to.

If you want to, the how is simple. If you want to, the way is simply *to do it.* First, you move past your little self feelings of regret, antagonism, and rebellion. Second, you move on from mental patterns formulated in the past which declare that there is no way to say thank you for happenings which you determine to be unacceptable; third, you move wholly into Higher Self and make the choice to offer praise and thanksgiving. The only requirement is that you mean it. A perfunctory or unenthusiastic thank you won't work.

If you want to direct love to your dis-ease, it needs to be all or nothing. You can fool some of the people some of the time, but yourself, never. When I say praise, I mean that you are to *rejoice* in the gift you've been given—in the same way you would respond to something you consciously sought, asked for, and received. Ironically, you also sought, asked for, and received your dis-ease—though most likely you did so unconsciously.

If you wept because you were stricken, weep now in your gratitude. If you complained about your dis-ease, openly and energetically, praise it now.

If you are still responding with the thought and the feeling (re-mind's old pattern and little self's response to that pattern), "This is impossible to do," then know this. Whether it is possible or impossible is simply a matter of choice—yours. I know, because I have chosen to know that it *is* possible. What about you?

Offering praise and thanksgiving, and directing love energy is the task before you in the void. You are sitting in the womb of life awaiting your delivery. The past is done, the future as yet unknown. You are marking time in the now listening to the beat of the creational process.

You are being nurtured by the placenta of new possibilities. You do not yet know the hour or moment of your emergence or what your shape will be, what shape you will be in.

You are forming, reforming. Approach the new with expectancy; hope and wait. Do not impose any limitations on yourself—no timetable, no fixed view of how you want to be, no specific to strive toward. Let your goal be patient unfolding, let your timetable be open-ended. Utilize the void to alter old habits and thought patterns, to shake up beliefs, to form new definitions, to offer yourself new perspectives and possibilities.

Allow yourself to examine dis-ease and healing as terms affecting your life in this present moment. How you define each of these concepts will determine how each manifests in you. Here are some definitions to reflect on, to ponder, to stimulate your own assessment. They occurred to me and to others at various times. See what occurs to you as you read them.

DIS-EASE IS the breaking down of old patterns, the eating away at matter previously formed, the upsetting of the standard molecular structure—all in order that you might have a conscious experience of the evolutionary process in which the old deteriorates and falls away so that the new and more harmonious might come into being.

DIS-EASE IS overbalance in just one of the many parts of your being.

DIS-EASE IS the reflection in manifested form of your state of consciousness in any given moment. It is the visible evidence of the masculine-feminine energy interaction functioning in the midst of creative unrest. It is the breakdown of the old in order that there might be the breakthrough to the new.

DIS-EASE IS the drumbeat sounding in the silent forest, struck by the hand of the God-self being born anew in the agony of the ecstatic life process.

DIS-EASE IS critical illness; illness that is critical

of the methods you used to bring it about.

DIS-EASE IS misused energy focused on ego-self rather than God-self.

DIS-EASE IS a malfunction of the whole self manifesting itself in the weakest part.

DIS-EASE IS like the sound track of a film running garbled or out of sync. If allowed to continue, it can eventually make a silent movie of one that was intended to be a talkie.

DIS-EASE IS the body's untempered revolt against tyrannical enslavement of the mind.

DIS-EASE IS the glorious disturbance of the status quo which, through pain and debilitation, shatters your patterns of living and forces you to let go of your demands and to hear instead your inner commands.

DIS-EASE IS yesterday's dirty wash being put through the wringer with the hope that enough of the fabric will be left to be worn in the sunshine of new life.

DIS-EASE IS your privileged opportunity to feel better.

DIS-EASE IS an inner earthquake instantly affecting some portion of your terrain, breaking up old sediments, leaving gaps to be filled with new configurations, causing havoc among individual cells scrambling for the harmony represented by the whole picture. The aftershocks are the ramifications that become clear only long after the initial blow to your little self has been sufficiently received and dealt with.

What is dis-ease to you? How do you now define it? How does your present view differ from your view before you were stricken? Are you satisfied with your definition? Are you open to change? Remember that how you define dis-ease in general directly affects your specific dis-ease and its healing.

Defining healing is equally important, and especially while you are allowing yourself reflective and still time in the void.

HEALING IS being willing to receive both dis-ease and healthfulness as holy.

HEALING IS being able to look back at the pain you experienced and feel good about it.

HEALING IS protecting your own Achilles' heel and being gentle with someone else's.

HEALING IS being the change you want to see happen until it actually does.

HEALING IS the metamorphosis of will-imposition into willing-submission. It is saying, "Yes," to what you said, "No," to and, "No," to what you said, "Yes," to. It is bringing into being a holy aggregation to replace the self-perpetuated aggravation.

HEALING IS being true to who you know you are, rather than fighting to become what you think you might be.

What is healing to you? Once you are able to state what it is for you, you can get on with doing it, with becoming it. Let your inner self guide you in the healing of your outer self.

The void is the rest stop after long stretches on

the hot, dusty road of a given cycle of life. It is the place where you can empty the bladder of your psyche and eliminate outdated concepts by moving the bowels of your being. The void is the place where you can take stock of where you've come from, and check your map to be sure that you know where you are going.

The void is the center in which you prepare for the new reality you will create for your new self. It is what you walk into when you move fully out of the past, and where you ready yourself to walk into the new that awaits your conscious acknowledgment.

Your time in the void is unpredictable and individual. It varies in duration for every sufferer of every dis-ease. Only you will know when you are ready to move beyond it and into the new. Only when you have finished with the void will the new become apparent. Only when you are willing to perceive and welcome the new will you be able to get on with it

7

GETTING ON WITH THE NEW: PROVIDING YOURSELF AND OTHERS WITH THE OPPORTUNITY TO GIVE TO YOU

Let's reflect on the fact that the act of *forgiving* is a truly unique opportunity for the giving of self to yourself and to others—*for giving* freely what you previously withheld grudgingly. Acknowledging this turns the concept of forgiving around just enough for you to see the inside of what is meant by the word in its deepest sense.

If someone has, or if you have, done something to yourself so terrible and painful that you are unable (or more precisely, unwilling) to forgive the other or the part of yourself that *you* hold responsible, what you have done in effect is frozen yourself in the moment when the act occurred and held yourself imprisoned in it. You have created a block in the flow of your love energy.

Your inner channel of being is a long corridor running through the whole of you. Along the way, dividers are available to be pulled out and snapped across the walls of the corridor, closing off a particular section at will, rendering it impassable and impenetrable. On the one hand, a closed section is clearly a safety area, an immunization section, which holds the energy in a fixed state and allows you to deal with the feeling or emotion more purely than if it were rushing through the whole of your inner corridor. On the other hand, it is a blockage like an air bubble, drawing your attention to it constantly because of the intensity of concentration you invest in it, and, therefore, greatly affecting your responses and actions in general. It is the inner core of disturbance which outwardly manifests itself in physical, spiritual, emotional, or mental dis-ease.

To forgive yourself or the other person is to release them from the trap you've snared them in and simultaneously to release yourself by opening the dividers and allowing your love energy to flow through you. The energy you've held frozen is the energy available for giving to yourself and to others.

When you have begun to give, you will begin to receive. As you give out energy, you open the way for more to come in. As the process accelerates to a pace that is normal and harmonious for you, good health (God-health) returns. God is love; love is unblocked energy. Unblocked energy is life in its purest form.

Forgiving is an excellent way to rid your system

of residuals which seem desirable in the short view but are highly taxable in the long run. Residual feelings keep you from living in the here and now. Residual deposits of calcium or fat result in a clogging up or hardening in the flow of your physical life. Residuals are excesses, like too much food, liquor, drugs, tobacco. They overload and incapacitate you. Residuals are *for giving* up to make room for the new which, when allowed and welcomed, will cascade through your energy system like high, cool waterfalls tumbling into a sun-streaked, dense forest.

Getting on with the new is easily facilitated by *forgiving*. By refusing to forgive, you are holding back energy. When you forgive, you release energy and let it flow unblocked. Therefore, forgiving is a way of setting healing energy in motion. Healing is energy *for giving* to yourself! What have you to give to yourself and others right now? What section of your energy system needs to be opened? What excess needs to be eliminated or set free? What grudges are you holding? What feelings are you harboring? Are you willing to expend what you have stored *for giving?* Are you willing to *forgive* yourself and others?

Take your time with this process. Walk down that inner corridor slowly. Let go with each step you take. Don't fool yourself into *thinking* that you have forgiven. This is a process of the heart center, overseen by choice, enacted throughout your being. This is to be done in deed, as well as in thought.

If a particular person is involved, you may want to go beyond simply releasing your hold on the interaction between you. You might want to pick up the phone, call that person, and say so. Let the love pass from you to him or her. Let the tears flow from you. Let your pride be replaced by holiness.

Is your re-mind telling you that it is too hard to do that? That it is too difficult to call another and say, "I forgive you for what you did," or, "I'm sorry for what I did or said," or, "For the ill will I harbored toward you." Ask yourself (your re-mind) if it is any easier to store it within you, to cripple yourself with it, to allow the excess to harden in you and barricade you from access to the open road of your life. Difficulty is only a matter of degree.

Only *you* will know when you have effected the complete release of a feeling, a person, an old reaction. You will experience the opening of a floodgate as if you were perspiring in a sauna, as if you were letting the juices flow in uninhibited sexual expression, as if you were letting out your breath after being under water, or as if you were jogging downhill in the cool of the morning.

Take the time now *for giving.*

When you give to yourself in this way, you invite those you have released to give *to* you—of the special gifts and talents they have to offer out of their uniqueness, of their love and compassion, of their energy. When you provide others with the opportunity to give to you, you are engaging in the greatest form of giving there is—that of receiving from others. By receiving from others, you give to them by acknowledging them. When you provide others with the opportunity to give, you act from strength, for you are initiating a transaction in which something new may be brought into manifestation. Thus you are mirroring the process by which the God-force brought everything on this plane of consciousness into being. That is highly appropriate for one such as yourself, who was made in the image of the Creator, for you are the reflector in manifestation of that Force.

When you provide others with the opportunity to give to you, you are reaching out to each according to his/her ability from each according to his/her need. Therein lies a harmonious economy in which the giver and receiver are equally blessed, equally activated, and equally filled.

By providing others with the opportunity to give to you, you are calling forth creativity and goodness. You are restoring your soul so that your cup may once again run over as you give to others who provide you with the opportunity to give to them.

You activate the new in you through the input of others. One of those "others" is your own Higher Self. It can give to you by asking pertinent questions and providing you with the opportunity to look deep into yourself and your condition in order that you might make stimulating choices about getting on with the new.

Get a pencil and paper and engage with yourself for a few moments. We're going to explore the dis-ease and see where you are with it at this very moment. Don't call up ideas about where you used to be with it; we want to move forward, not backward. To bring into consciousness what's going on with you *right now* is to actively engage in healing.

How would you define your condition? Is it affecting you physically, mentally, spiritually, emotionally, or in a combination of these? Write down your responses and be sure to put a date on the paper. Tomorrow you may feel differently. Of the four categories I mentioned, which is the most pronounced? What does that mean to you? How hopeful are you about your ability to restore your health?

How do you perceive your condition as having begun? Did someone say something that set the sparks flying in you? Was it in that exact moment that the dis-ease began? Or, was it that the condition you are now experiencing actually had deep roots in childhood which have only now surfaced in this current manifestation? For example, are you suffering from a feeling of being unworthy of your family's love and attention and did this condition actually begin when you were very little and you sat wide-eyed in church hearing the minister say that YOU were born in sin!? Is that what has manifested now?

To what exactly do you trace your condition? To some specific occurrence? To someone else whom you caught it from? To your own giving up and inviting the dis-ease in?

Was there a specific event with which it coincided or which it followed? For example, did someone you love deeply tell you a sudden and final-sounding goodbye? In that moment did you experience blinding tears in your eyes which went unshed, a lump in your throat, a knot in your stomach, a rush or swift fall of energy in your heart? Was this followed later (days, weeks, months) by deep, unexplainable depression; by a seemingly uncaused difficulty in swallowing, an ulcer or colitis or other stomach trouble; a heart attack or arterial blockage; visual impairment?

You may trace a broken leg to the day you actually broke the bone, to the event of falling or being in the accident. However, it may be that the event began well before the seeming incident, when you broke a promise to yourself or broke the free flow of your energy by restricting yourself with blocks.

Each time you respond to these questions, your answers may be different because of new insights and a new willingness to see other possibilities.

How do you feel about this condition? About having it? About yourself in relation to it? What would you like in relation to it?

After you've written your responses, your true, uncensored feelings, remember that you are not glued to them. They are of the moment and subject to change with each new moment.

After you've written them, reread them. As you look into them, see what you are bringing into being. Are you aggravating your condition by the feelings you create? Are your feelings serving to cleanse you, as if they were an antiseptic energy wash for your little self to use as a gargle? Feel what you are feeling and then be done with the feeling. Spit out the gargle when you are finished.

The questions I ask you now are the same ones I asked you earlier in different ways. You hear and see on a slightly altered plane each time the same ground is covered. Illness, healing, life itself are all variations on a theme, varied ramifications of the same basic essence. The questions I asked you earlier, the concepts we reflected on together, were used then to identify where you were then. The same ones are relevant now, and so it is at each step of the way.

Processes by which insights are gained may be used in the midst of dis-ease, on the road to recovery, in retrospect of the healing, and even in preparation for being newly stricken! This is by way of saying that I'm not offering you any magic. Tricks don't last very long. I am offering you a means through which an in-depth search may be more easily facilitated in your everyday life.

Whip out your pencil again and give yourself some more answers. When you talk about your condition to others or think about it to yourself, how do you describe it? What words, phrases, expressions do you use? Have they changed any since you began reading this handbook? Are they expressions that hold you locked into the dis-ease, or do they reflect only what you know to be true in the here and now? Are you beginning to utilize phrases that, by their very nature, move you to the new, guide you to harmony?

Check on your responses, on the words you used to define your condition as of today. If you are not satisfied with any of them, change them right now. The way you get on with the new is to bring it into being by word and deed. When you recognize that what you've said is irrelevant or limiting, change it instantly to what is meaningful and expanding. Only you can do that for yourself.

As a specific means of getting on with the new, I would like to put another series of questions to you. They are based on the principles of The Love Project, a way of life through which Seekers may tap their highest and best and be more fully loving to themselves and those around them. I introduced them to you at the start of this book when I introduced myself to you. I've also been using them as many of the chapter headings. Officially they are:

Receive all persons as beautiful exactly where they are.

Create your own reality consciously, rather than living as if you have no control over your life.

Have no expectations, but rather abundant expectancy.

Be the change you want to see happen, instead of trying to change everyone else.

Provide others with the opportunity to give.

Perceive problems as opportunities.

Remember: Choice is the life process. In every new moment of awareness, you are free to make a new choice.

These principles have been powerful life-changing agents for me and for thousands of others to whom they have been introduced since 1970.

When they were given to me, just after I had made the commitment to live a life of love, I was teaching in a ghetto high school in Brooklyn, New York. Human relations were hardly in existence in the school at the time. The 4500 black and brown students had very little loving communication going on with the 225 faculty members, mostly white. Students lived in rat- and roach-infested apartments. Many went hungry and were ill-clothed in the midst of winter. There were problems with reading, with attendance, with drug overdoses, with violence. The neighborhood was lined with garbage and partially burned out and abandoned buildings. The situation seemed hopeless. (And you think you've got it bad? Check again.)

It was under these circumstances that I offered myself to the universe as a carrier of the staff of love and began to set healing energy in motion in a school suffering from incredible social dis-ease.

The Love Project principles represented the medicine used by physicians of love (students, teachers and administrators) who joined with me in ministering in a new way to alleviate the suffering around us.

Within seven months a miracle had taken place. The energy configuration of the environment of the school had been altered so greatly that it was almost impossible not to notice. What had been a hell-hole of violence and negativity was now a center of love and caring. Students were smiling at each other, engaging in personal and community activities together, organizing major events and joyful demonstrations. Students and teachers shared more openly and worked side by side in creative endeavors. Reading improved and the population at the school library increased as a result of give-away book festivals. A spirit of cooperation permeated the entire environment. A healing had taken place. How? Through a series of love-centered activities and the principles of The Love Project.

I offer the principles of The Love Project to you now for *your* healing. They were gifts from my Higher Self to me when I was ready to set healing energy in motion in my life. Perhaps your Higher Self will speak to you through them now.

The most important thing about these principles is that they are for each of us to be and to do in and through ourselves. They are not for us to tell others to use so that we can get along with them better. They are a way of being.

I offer them to you now in the form of questions in order that you might become more aware of what you are being and doing and how this relates to the dis-ease you are seeking to bring into harmony.

The questions I put to you are simple. The more intense your reflection on them, the more profound your responses to yourself will be. Write full-sentence answers so that you can go back to them later to reflect on what you have written.

1. In general, do you receive yourself as beautiful exactly where you are, or do you put yourself down? Do you like who you are? Do you love who you are? Do you like yourself enough to invest energy in healing yourself? Are you willing to let your ship sink because you've rejected your cargo?

   Do you receive yourself as beautiful in relation to your dis-ease? Are you willing to give yourself a chance, or are you poisoning yourself with overdoses of negativity ingested frequently?

Once again, your answers to these questions today will tell you exactly where you are in your healing process. You may want to ask them again tomorrow or next week to see how you've grown or changed. And when and if you are fully well, ask them of yourself again, and again, for they will help you to remain well. For now, we'll focus on using them to bring the new into being.

2. Have you created the reality of your dis-ease consciously? What *were* you conscious of doing? What reality would you now *like* to create?
3. Do you have expectations in relation to your

condition? Do you have expectations in relation to yourself and being able to do something about it? Do you have them in relation to life in general, or do you let things happen and then interact with them? If you have expectations, are you willing to let go of them?

Do you have your mind set on *the way* to get better? Or on *getting* better (or being healed) at all? Have you left yourself open to unthought-of possibilities?

Are your answers different now than when you probed your expectations in the last chapter?

4. How can you *be* the change you want to see happen? How can you *be* the new you you want to bring into being?
5. Do you provide others with the opportunity to give to you? In what specific ways? In relation to healing? In relation to the new you you want to bring into being? Can you receive from another without feeling guilty about getting? Are you worthy to receive?
6. What opportunities are you providing yourself with through this dis-ease? You may want to reiterate what you thought of before or you may come up with totally new ideas if you are willing to open yourself anew in this moment. Expressions of speech and parts of the body may give you clues now, as they did before, as to what the opportunities are. Let your thoughts run free and see what you come up with in this fresh exploration.

Using a physical condition affecting the back as an example, let every expression you can think of in relation to backs come into your consciousness, and write them down. Some examples: holding back, backtrack, in back of me, back up, back down, back and forth, backstage, front to back, get your back up, flashback, back away, backing, back debts, backslapper, never turn back, I want you back, hunchback, call back, left back, backlash, backlog, horseback, on my back, back to nature, aching back, back to back, get off my back, monkey on my back, a comeback, backbreaking, halfback. Now, look back over all the expressions. What stands out for you? What connections can you make? What clues are you giving yourself in relation to the new you you can now bring into being. Earlier you were looking into expressions like this in order to move beyond the problem dimension. Now you are using the same process to spread the new before you.

As an example, rather than focusing on how you held back in the past, now you can specifically zero in on the many ways in which you can actively let go. You can release premises, expectations, persons, feelings, thoughts, desires. If holding back had been a full-time job with you, letting go will be equally full in that it requires conscious awareness on your part in the midst of life situations. If a friend expresses an opinion to you and you feel pained by the expression, you can practice letting go in the midst of that exchange; if you are holding back, make a new choice to express what you are feeling.

What may have happened in the past is that you held back and were not aware of it until later when you discovered you were still holding a knot of tension in your stomach (or your back) as a carry-over from the exchange. The new reality you can begin to create is to be aware of this process while in the midst of holding back—to nip it in the bud, to release the energy in the instant you feel yourself holding on to it, to *say* what you are feeling instead of feeling what you are unwilling to say.

This is a sample of the kind of process you can engage in with yourself in relation to one or more expressions about your condition that speak to you of the way opening to the new.

Metaphors are yet another excellent means of getting a glimpse of the new that awaits you. They are just mysterious enough to be poetic and offbeat, and thus to stir a new direction toward an intuitive plane. They enable you to take one step beyond yourself so that you may look back at who you are from the new perspective. You align yourself with an image apart from yourself which runs parallel to you and therefore affords you a detached look from an objective viewing point.

As in the case of the back condition, some metaphors you might offer yourself are:

It is as if the bottom of my spine were a forked road or tongue.

It is as if my spinal cord were hanging loose, looking for footing.

It is as if I were a string of uncooked spaghetti

that would break if bent, or would yield if cooked (if altered).

It is as if an organ pedal at the core of my soul were being pushed constantly.

It is as if a massive tree were breaking through stone to reach for the sun.

It is as if a slingshot or bow were pulled back to the fullest and ready to spring.

After you have let a string of images and as-ifs flow through you, review them all to see what theme runs through them. What is clear in the samples recorded above is that the new is waiting, and is right on the brink of coming into being, pointing to a direction that is clearly a different mode of expression. The forked road, the cord looking for a footing, yielding and altering, reaching, ready to spring. The new is almost unwilling to wait any longer; hence the tension has built to a breaking point in the back.

To discover what new is actually waiting, it would be well to examine what you've been resisting, delaying, pushing aside. If you did so, because you were afraid to risk the new, you might ask yourself if it's worth it to continue suffering in the now in an effort to hold off a possible suffering in the future, about which you have no guarantees. Seems as if you risk more by killing yourself in the safety of non-risking than you do in stepping out into an unknown that might be far less hurting than you now project. Oddly enough, the pain you project as possible in some future risk clearly comes from the *now* in which it is being experienced. It seems silly not to go ahead, since what you are attempting to prevent is already happening. It has to do with where you are and not necessarily with where you're going.

Conversations with self are the most enlightening you can have. Write a dialogue between yourself and the metaphor. Speak to it and invite it to speak to you. Talk to it as you would a friend or advisor; write the dialogue out as if you were two characters in a play. Do the same with you and your dis-ease, with you and the future, with you and your past. The combinations are endless, and equally so will be the resulting insights.

Getting on with the new begins with getting as deeply as possible into the now. The one thing you've given yourself is time. Use it.

8

RECEIVING YOURSELF AS BEAUTIFUL EXACTLY AS YOU ARE

It's time to get down to some nitty-gritty matters. It's fine to talk about recovery and healing as if no remnants will remain, as if all will be as it was or better, as if wholeness will be restored. In such eventualities, it is much easier to receive yourself as beautiful exactly where you are.

Perhaps, before I go on, it would be helpful if I defined the terminology I just used in a little more detail. *To receive* means to let flow through you or to breathe in and through yourself. It has nothing to do with accepting. If you *accept* yourself, you need first *to judge* that you are acceptable. *Receiving is not a matter of judging.* It also has nothing to do with how you *feel* about it. You can feel terrible and still *receive* if you put up no blocks to yourself and thus allow your whole self into consciousness. *As beautiful* means *in perfection.* It means that exactly as you are, you are in perfection, fulfilling the task assigned you by the universe as your role in the overall. When you are succeeding, you are beautiful; when you are failing, you are beautiful. The same is true when you are struggling, loving, fighting, caring, dying, giving up, coming out on top. *Is*ness is beautiful. People strive for perfection because they perceive it as an end-state rather than as a process which is ongoing. People view perfection as impossible to reach because they have no idea that they are already in it. They are speaking truth when they say it's impossible to *reach,* yet they have arrived at that truth through erroneous reasons and thus have missed the point.

Receiving yourself as beautiful is a concert conducted by your Higher Self using the musicians of your heart center to play a symphony of universal love. Energy pouring into or out of the heart center is devoid of judgments, opinions, thoughts. It is like strains of music that permeate the great music hall of life and resound in the echoes of timelessness. It is in this environment that the note of yourself is sounded and received in its perfection.

It first dawned on me to receive myself as beautiful after seeing a movie in which the entire population of the earth, except for a handful of people, were killed in a nuclear holocaust. As I sat watching I thought to myself, "What if *I* were the only person left on earth and I didn't like myself?" Can you imagine being stuck with someone you didn't like, and especially yourself!? I didn't consider it funny, particularly because of how much energy I was investing in self-criticism at that time. If I had been forced to live with only me, I would have been miserable. I would have moved out.

Right then and there I began to shift gears. I began to express appreciation for myself, to like myself, actually to delight in myself. If I were going to be the last person on earth, at least I would be a joy to be with. I received myself as beautiful and I've been doing it ever since. I really enjoy me. After all, if I don't, who will? I laugh at my own jokes. I praise my efforts. I appreciate the fine work I do. I delight in my smile. I'm one of my favorite people to hug.

Receiving yourself as beautiful exactly where you are is a matter of choice. It's time we found out what choices you are making in this regard.

Has your doctor told you that you can be assured of a full recovery after a time? Are you waiting until then to receive yourself as beautiful? If you're not receiving yourself now, what are you doing? Are you putting yourself down as helpless? That will only further the creation of helplessness. Are you beating up on yourself for being in this position in the first place? That's a great way to keep yourself in it even longer. Are you seeing yourself as half a person and thus overlooking the half of you that awaits your acknowledgment? Are you trying to replace receiving yourself with feeling sorry for yourself? Are you aware that feeling sorry for yourself is a masked way of rejecting yourself through self-imposed impotence?

If you have been receiving yourself as beautiful exactly where you are, you probably are rejoicing in the healing process as it is taking place in you, experiencing the wonder of being pregnant with new cells readying for birth in new wholeness. You probably are expressing gratitude for the time you've been given to patch the tears in the fabric of your being. You probably are extolling the virtues of the self of yourself who had wisdom enough to stop in time.

Have you been told that you won't be able to drive any more, that you can't have any more children, that you are going to be expelled, that your credit has been denied, that your references proved unsatisfactory, that you are being evicted, that you don't qualify, that you're past your prime, that you have to retire, that you're not wanted in the club, that you can't measure up to the rest of the team, that you're never to call again, that you've been replaced?

Have you been told that there will be no full recovery; that you will always walk with a limp; will never be able to run again; will lose a breast; will be on medication for the rest of your life; will be paralyzed on one side of your body; will be totally blind; will need a wheelchair; will not regain your memory; will be disfigured for life; will always be on a special diet?

What was your response when you were told that you would be disabled or rejected in a particular way? Were you angry, thrust into despair, depleted? Did you weep? Did you stop breathing and create a block in your being? Did you rise to fight against the verdict? Did you wish you were dead?

The larger and more important question is, did you receive (are you receiving) yourself as beautiful right in the midst of being handed the most difficult news you might ever have to hear?

The first step is to receive the verdict; receive it without adding on to it a string of consequences that you predict will happen as a result. Receiving does not include playing the if-this-then-this game. If I am paralyzed on one side of my body, then I will no longer be able to walk, work, play golf, do anything the way I used to, etc. The list of projections could go on forever.

The point is that you don't know that the then-this will come to pass. And if it does, it's far easier to deal with when it happens than *before* it does, as you imagine it in your mind. When you project ahead of yourself you are thrusting yourself into a future you know nothing about. You say, "I won't be able to . . ." because at this point, in the here and now, you have no idea what your capabilities and resources will be then. Hence, to predict and project in this manner is wasted energy.

To *receive* the verdict, the prognosis, means that *you limit what you hear to what is being said!* (as differentiated from limiting yourself by taking on the prognosis).

"I am paralyzed on one side," is what you are

given to receive. Any more than that, namely, "and this means that" is to go beyond simply receiving.

Receiving the verdict as beautiful means that *even though* it hurts, *even though* you don't like it or want it, *even though* you don't understand it, you acknowledge that it is part of the perfection of your life as it is unfolding. You have been given a heavy burden to carry. You are capable of bearing it if you choose to. It is a challenge to new growth in you.

Receiving the verdict as beautiful means that you receive your feelings in relation to it as beautiful as well. Affirm yourself for not liking the fact that a skill or way of life you once had will no longer be yours. Your dissatisfaction will stimulate you to bring your life together in a new pattern of harmony. Be glad that you experience hurt so deeply. It is exactly that intensity of feeling that can be utilized in actively getting on with your life. Delight in the fact that you do not understand why you deserve this. Precisely because you don't understand and are troubled by your lack of understanding, you will pursue the matter, dig deeper into the meanings, and benefit from your findings.

The most profound aspect of receiving yourself as beautiful exactly where you are is receiving your newly acquired limitations, your newly limited self.

You cannot do what you once did. So? What are you going to do about that? Beat yourself to a pulp? Further limit yourself by conjuring up a limited view of your limitations? Do you want to shout? Go right ahead. Did you shout right out loud and get your energy moving? Or did you shout inside your body where no one would hear you but your own tissues? That's part of the way your disease may have come into being in the first place. You shouted at yourself and your body shouted right back by reflecting your shout in the breakdown of matter. It said loud and clear, "Look, this is the impact on me of the violence with which you struck."

You now have limitations! What's new about that? You had them before you were stricken—different ones than you now have, but you had limitations all the same. Exploring what they were might help to put your newly acquired ones into perspective. Could you not run very fast, touch your toes, swim 50 laps? Could you not cope with emotional upset, handle financial matters, tell people to back off when you didn't want to see them? What *were* your limitations? Did you learn to live with them? Did you simply focus on what you *could do* and pour your energy into that? Did you eventually not even see them as limitations, but rather as things you simply didn't do, didn't care to develop?

Now you have some other limitations. *Process them.* First acknowledge that you have them; then receive them as beautiful and incorporate them into your life with the rest of your limitations.

As a result of your dis-ease you have engaged in a trade-in. You have given up prior skills in order that you might gain new awareness. It was not necessarily essential that you give up anything to achieve the new, but that *is* the way you did it. Perhaps it *was* necessary for you.

It is important to remember that you are in a new relationship with yourself. Out of new limitations imposed on your old self, your new awareness will allow for the emergence of your new self. You've heard all the old stories of people who lose their sight and improve the capacity of their other senses about one hundred percent, stories of people who lose their right arms and end up playing better golf than ever before due to the concentrated strength and control they develop in their left arms, or stories about women who have lost their husbands and opened doors to incredible careers for themselves as a way of dealing with the necessities of life.

Place your focus where it belongs! Place it on what you *can* do right now, not on what you are no longer able to do. You are not disabled; you are *otherwise abled.* Acquaint yourself with how, and begin building from there.

Your limitations may or may not be lasting. Clearly, you are restricted now. This does not necessarily mean that you always will be. Utilize the word "yet" often. Say, "I can't, yet." Leave the door open to further healing in the future.

An excellent way to practice receiving yourself and your limitations as beautiful is to receive others in the same way. Zero in on friends and family. What don't you like about them? Practice affirming them and the qualities in them that you would prefer not having in yourself. Receive them with love no matter what they do or say. How can you do that? Simply by wanting to. Receive yourself in the same way. Want to.

This chapter is a brief one. That's because limitations play a very small role in your life. That is, unless *you* overemphasize them. You could build them up into the most important part of your life. You could let them take over. The choice is yours.

9

REBIRTH: BE THE CHANGE YOU WANT TO SEE HAPPEN

I trust you are familiar with the story of Aladdin and his fabulous lamp. All he had to do was rub it, and the genie would grant him three wishes. No products to buy, no obligations. Simply rub and wish.

Lest you mistakenly think that the genie is the sole hero in the process since he is the one who grants the wishes, consider this. If Aladdin had not known what he wanted, if he had not wished for what he wanted, the genie would have been powerless to give him anything.

In order for something to come into being, someone has to initiate the process.

When you were born, your mother and father did most of the initiating work. Probably they didn't see it as work when they began to bring you into being. When it comes to rebirth, to allowing a healthy self to emerge out of the ashes of your disease, the process is up to you. You are the one with the wishes and you are the genie in the lamp. You are the mother and father of your new wholeness. You can perceive the process as work, or as a delight and privilege.

The you I am speaking about is your Higher Self. It is the overseer that knows all. Your Higher Self is your observer self. It watches your actions. It holds before you *awareness* of what you are doing and invites you to become *conscious* of what you are doing.

Through your Higher Self you can see you—body, re-mind and little self—move about in the midst of living. Your Higher Self lives *through* your body, not *in* it. When you choose to become conscious of your Higher Self, you provide yourself with a focal point for your feelings, thoughts and sensations. Your Higher Self receives all messages you send it, and if you are willing to consult with it, it will provide you with ways to move through what you're dealing with, to keep energy flowing unblocked.

For example, if someone says something that hurts you, your Higher Self will be the first to tell you that it was you who created hurt in response to what was said and that you could make other choices instead. Your little self reacts with feelings; your re-mind reacts with judgments and opinions; your body registers the results of both.

Your Higher Self, as differentiated from these

three, *responds* rather than reacts. It moves, as if it were an akido expert, without resistance to the energy coming in. It dances with it. It lets it flow through, and then sends forth a harmonious energy configuration.

In the example of being hurt shared above, a Higher Self response might be simply to register what was said. To hear it without simultaneously registering a reaction to it. If you are hearing a statement and reacting to it at the same time, you run the risk of hearing *only* what *you* are hearing and never actually receiving what the other person is saying.

As another example, you might be in the presence of someone suffering from a bad cold. Your mind might feed you data that this illness is contagious and therefore you will catch the cold. Your body might begin to sneeze and your little self might begin to feel anxious. In this instance, your Higher Self would observe and report to you that B does not necessarily follow A. Just because the person with whom you are conversing has need of a cold to cleanse out unexpressed feelings, does not mean that you need to bring that condition into manifestation in yourself. *Your most powerful immunization is your ability to know what you have no need of in a given moment.* If you allow the configuration of dis-ease to pass on through, offering it no invitation to take up residence through doubt, fear, or sureness that you will catch it, you will not create the cold in you.

Your Higher Self gives you a view of the whole

so that any action you take will not be unduly influenced by any single facet of yourself. It enables you to see yourself in the midst of a process, to watch how you are relating, and to make new choices midstream.

Paying heed to your Higher Self is your opportunity to talk with yourself *before,* and *as,* you are bringing a reality into being. This is certainly easier than and preferable to causing yourself to be stricken by a condition and talking to yourself *through it* and after it.

The Higher Self is where responses originate. When you proceed in life situations with those responses, you are bringing newness into being. You are *being* the change you want to see happen. This is very different from investing energy in trying to change other people, trying to convince them to do what you want.

Being the change begins with consciously registering the state of being in which you are functioning. If you are not pleased with what you register, you are stirred to bring change about. If the stirring occurs in your re-mind, you think and ponder about the possible changes. If your little self is stirred, your wants and desires are evoked. Your Higher Self can provide you with the means to bring the thoughts and desires into being. The *how* is simple, do it!

When I say *do it,* I mean just that. Do it all the way. Don't be deterred by anything. Pour your energy concentration into bringing the new reality into being, into being the change you want to see happen.

Let me give you an example of the total application I mean. When I was fourteen and in my sophomore year at the High School of Performing Arts in New York, I spoke with a very heavy Brooklyn accent. I sounded like a stereotype. In addition, I spoke incredibly fast. My teacher told me that unless I did some work on my speech I would be exceedingly limited in terms of the roles I hoped to play in the future in the theater. It was clear that I had to make a change. In effect, I needed to heal a dis-ease, a disharmony, in my speech pattern.

First, I made the choice to do it. Second, I looked at all the sounds that were out of harmony. Next, I learned the entire phonetic alphabet and how every sound would be pronounced perfectly in Eastern Standard Speech. Then, I was ready actually to *do* the change.

For the next two and a half weeks, I did not utter a single sound unless it was pronounced perfectly. Each time I opened my mouth, I formed the sounds as I knew they were to be made and then sent them out. I did this in the midst of my life—at home, on the street, with my friends, in ordinary conversation. Perhaps the most painful times were in my classes. I'd be called on to give an answer and it would take three to five minutes to put the proper sounds together in sentences.

People responded to me with wonder, annoyance, amazement, ridicule, irritation, encouragement. One of my tasks was to remain clear of what others thought or felt about what I was doing. *They* were not doing it and therefore their reactions were not relevant—only mine were. I was delighting in myself. I was doing what I had set out to do. It was hard, but I was doing it. The first week was horrendous. During the second week, things got better. At the end of two and one-half weeks, I had entirely changed my speech pattern and was speaking naturally. It was incredible. It was hard for others to believe or even adjust to.

Having once made such a radical change consciously, I never had any question later in my life about being able to accomplish that quality of change at any time in relation to anything. I had learned that nothing is fixed, unless I continue to hold it in place. Everything is energy and in a state of flux. Through my guidance of the change process, I can bring the new into being by simply doing it.

You have been registering in your consciousness your state of being during this time of dis-ease. You are not pleased. You want change to take place. Exactly *what* change do you want? That's the first step to activating the genie.

What you *want* needs to be phrased in positive terms. To say "I want to stop the pain in my joints" says nothing about what you *want* to bring into being. It speaks of stopping, not starting. In this case your objective might be stated as:

1. To move with greater harmony
2. To facilitate flexibility
3. To walk with ease

Your objective, then, should always be a clear statement of the change you want to see happen.

Formulate one for your particular condition, that is:

4. To breathe freely, unobstructed
5. To strengthen my heart
6. To build a new life as a single person
7. To trust people
8. To love my body even though it's been radically altered
9. To regain sight or hearing
10. To stimulate movement in my paralyzed limbs

Once you have clearly defined your objective, turn your attention to what you perceive your obstacles to be. What stands in the way of your achieving your objective?

You might be wondering why I am asking you to think of obstacles. It would seem you'd have enough to do pouring energy into your objective. The reason is simple. By calling them up into consciousness, you leave no hidden adversaries lying in wait to leap out at you at will. There are obstacles to everything, whether they are real or imagined (and in truth those words are interchangeable, given the nature of the universe), and they serve an important function. Just as you would be hard pressed to have electricity without positive and negative ions, so you'd not get very far if you had an objective devoid of a spark to ignite your initiative to bring it into being. That is the function of the obstacle. It is your stepping stone to fulfilling your objective. It is a negative charge box which can set in motion your positively stated objective. Because it tells you no, you are actively stimulated to find a way to effect a yes.

As obstacles to 1, 2, and 3, above, I might say my arthritis stands in my way, or the pain is too severe to attempt it, or I'm too crippled already.

As to the other sample obstacles:

4. My lungs are too congested.
5. I haven't the energy.
6. I don't want to live alone.
7. People are untrustworthy.
8. My body is scarred, maimed, deformed.
9. I have no power over my eyes or ears.
10. The nerves are dead.

Allow your obstacles to come from your deepest worries. Call up the most difficult hurdles you can imagine. The stronger the objective and the tougher the obstacle, the greater the thrust into action.

Now we come to a crucial step: What do you *do* to get what you want? What specific actions or activities can you do to bring about the change you want to see happen? These must be defined with active verbs, doing verbs.

I would not be moved into action if I began with phrases like "to try," "to attempt," "to plan." I would not be doing if I said, "I want to," or "I would like to." You might as well be saying, "to avoid," or "to postpone."

Allow the action to emerge from what you have defined as the obstacle, and refine it until it rings in harmony with the tone set forth in the objective.

I'll use the previously stated objectives and obstacles as examples. As practice, add your own actions to the ones I give you before moving on to deal with your own.

Objective: To move with greater harmony
Obstacle: My arthritis stands in my way
Actions: To exercise;
to rename the dis-ease and remove the stigma of the label (For example, instead of arthritis, you might call it unbendingness, or inflexibility, or reluctance or resistance to movement.)

Objective: To facilitate flexibility
Obstacle: The pain is too severe to attempt it
Actions: To breathe deeply;
to expand my tolerance for pain

Objective: To walk with ease
Obstacle: I'm too crippled already
Actions: To focus on what is still healthy tissue;
to view each tiny step forward as a great achievement

Objective: To breathe freely, unobstructed
Obstacle: My lungs are too congested
Actions: To inhale slowly, consciously;
to expel congestion each time I exhale

Objective: To strengthen my heart

Obstacle: I don't have the energy
Actions: To move as slowly as I need to;
to do only what I can; no more, no less

Objective: To build a new life as a single person
Obstacle: I don't want to live alone
Actions: To live with friends or relatives temporarily;
to do as a lone person what I did as part of a couple;
to focus on my own strengths and assets;
to grieve fully without cutting the process short

Objective: To trust people
Obstacle: People are untrustworthy
Actions: To be trustworthy myself;
to practice risking in little unimportant areas first;
to forgive those who failed to meet *my* expectations

Objective: To love my body even though it's been radically altered
Obstacle: My body is scarred, maimed, deformed
Actions: To look at me, rather than try to hide me;
to be tender with my body and not further traumatize it;

to find beauty in what my little self fears is ugly to others;
to delight in what is healthy in me

Objective: To regain sight or hearing
Obstacle: I have no power over my eyes or ears
Actions: To seek out new ways to see or hear by activating other senses;
to seek understanding from those in similar positions

Objective: To stimulate movement in my paralyzed limbs
Obstacle: The nerves are dead
Actions: To direct my attention to the site of breakage where the skill was lost and invite the cells of my body to regenerate the missing link;
to actively rub those limbs

Actions are to be changed as often as diapers. They should be simple and to the point. As soon as they accomplish what they set out to, they are to be modified or replaced so that newer and more relevant ones might be brought into focus.

As the actions change, the objective will also be modified, as will the obstacle. By being the change you want to see happen, you are seeing directly into the life-process and bringing about rebirth in yourself.

You are being allowed into the womb of a

healing pregnancy. You are being invited to give birth to a different self, to a change in you. When the change has been born, you will not only be the new baby, you will have been cognizant of the birth process, engaged in by you as the emerging fetus, and you will have been the parent of your new self.

Perhaps it would be good to practice, as with the previous samples, with a few other examples. Just like developing your opportunity muscle, the more you practice with defining objectives, pinpointing and routing out obstacles, and stating actions that are doable, the better you will become at it. You will find that you'll be able to apply this technique to almost everything.

Practice with the samples that follow by adding to the actions I offer as suggestions. Conjure up as many as you can, focusing always on being increasingly specific.

Objective	***Obstacle***	***Actions***
1) To release my former mate	a) I hate him /her	a) To forgive myself and my mate
	b) The divorce was his/her fault, not mine	b) To love *myself* more actively
		c) To affirm my worth in everything I do

Objective	*Obstacle*	*Actions*
2) To move beyond my need for smoking	a) I'm addicted	a) To practice deep breathing and filling myself without needing smoke to do it b) to focus on my needs in each moment and not function out of habit
3) To find a person with whom to share my life	a) I'm afraid of being rejected or hurt b) I'm not sure there is one	a) To open myself to the unexpected b) To be the the kind of person I want to attract to me c) To tell others that I'm looking

Objective	***Obstacle***	***Actions***
4) To be worthy of a raise or a promotion	a) I'm too shy to ask b) Others have been there longer than I have	a) To focus on being highly creative in my work b) To voice constructive opinions whenever I have an idea c) To help others around me as much as possible
5) To be more outgoing and expressive	a) I don't know how b) Others will think I'm crazy c) I haven't much to offer	a) To invest more focused energy in the little things I do each day b) To speak without thinking c) To laugh louder and more often d) To ask ex-

Objective	*Obstacle*	*Actions*
		pressive people how they do it e) To affirm that what I see as expressive in others is potential in me or I wouldn't recognize it in them
6) To be free of excessive responsibilities	a) I've already committed myself b) I'll feel guilty if I cut out on people	a) To give myself permission to reevaluate any part of my life at any time b) To practice saying "no" more often c) To provide others with the opportunity to help me out from under

Carefully defining your process in this way is very helpful in terms of bringing the new into focus, into the realm of the possible and eventually, into being.

There are other very effective ways to bring the new into being. One is through sound. Go into your room and close the door. Stand with your eyes closed, open your mouth wide, take a deep breath and sound the lowest note your voice chooses to make. Let the sound fill you. Hear it inside yourself rather than with your outer ear or your critical re-mind. Breathe again. Let the sound out again. Repeat this until you are making the sound as fully, as richly, as loudly as possible, for five full minutes at the minimum.

Then, try other sounds. Move up and down the full range of sounds. Don't approach it as singing or scale work—*groan, moan, o-o-o-o* and *ah-h-h*. Allow yourself to feel the vibrations. Pull the sound down to the soles of your feet. Shoot it out through the top of your head. Find a sound that feels harmonious to you. Let it out of you, loud and clear. Be warmed by it, loved by it. Five or ten minutes here would prepare you well.

When you are sufficiently warmed up, stand in silence with your eyes closed and focus in on what you are experiencing as dis-ease. As you zero in on it, open your mouth, breathe deeply, and make what feels to you like the sound of dis-ease. If, when it emerges, it is not *exactly* the sound, try it again (and again) until you find what feels right to you. When you've got it, make the sound over and over again as loudly, as resonantly, as fully as you can, and for as long as you want to. Feel where the sound registers in your physical body. Envision the energy that is blocked there. Pull the sound into the area of dis-ease. Concentrate and focus on the size and shape of the dis-ease. See its color. Then thrust the sound out, and as you do so, shake up the configuration of the dis-ease. Repeat this often, pull in on the sound and concentrate; thrust out on the sound and shake up. Each time be aware that you are moving the energy (that the dis-ease is nothing more than energy to be moved and reutilized).

As a next step, allow your body to move with the sound. Let your movements express the energy of the dis-ease, just as the sound is doing. Over and over again, allow your sound and movement to express the dis-ease. Then breathe deeply several times with your eyes closed. This time when you make the sound of the dis-ease and move your body in the energy of the dis-ease, allow your voice and body to join league with your Higher Self to move the sound and the body from an expression of dis-ease to one that represents what would be harmony for you in this particular regard. Make the sound and the movement of wellness. Let the voice and the body shift freely from dis-ease to harmony.

Make sound-making and energetic movement a part of your day. Sound your harmony often. Practice lifting and moving energy on sound waves. Don't *watch* for your condition to change. Focus on *being* the change and let the rest happen naturally.

As with sound and movement, simple breathing is another way of *being* the change you want to see happen. Set aside time for *conscious* breathing as differentiated from what might be your ordinary shallow breathing-for-living.

Sit still with your back straight. Breathe in deeply. Breathe into the *center* of your dis-ease. Breathe out *through* it. Move the congested energy *on* the breath, letting go more and more as you exhale, taking in new life energy as you inhale.

One other approach to *being* the change is in the realm of color. Color is a visual reflection of a given vibration. The colors with which you surround yourself in clothing and home environment are a living canvas clearly depicting the quality of the energy in which you choose to live. For example, do you wear dark colors—blacks, deep browns, navy blues? These colors drink up energy, absorb it into *themselves.* Are you experiencing *yourself* as low on energy? Is the energy going into your clothes instead of being available to you? Yellows and oranges are often referred to as bright and perky. They bounce energy out and back to you rather than absorbing it for themselves.

Take time to review the colors you have chosen to live with, to live in. Examine how they make you feel—if they are producing effects which serve to intensify the dis-ease. If this is the case, bring a change into being with a can of paint or a shopping spree.

Being the change you want to see happen

doesn't take much—first see it, then be it!

Utilizing many of the techniques I've shared with you in this book, I have brought about incredible change in my own being. Not only have I healed emotional and mentally aggravating conditions but I have worked miracles in my physical body.

In 1961 I threw my back out and landed in the hospital unable to move without pain from the neck down. I was told by assorted doctors, then and throughout the next fifteen years of suffering with the condition, that nothing could be done to heal it and that I needed a support belt and had better wear one or I'd be a cripple before very long!

I didn't believe that. I acknowledged that the *doctors* believed it and that indeed they could *not* do anything for me. Then, I turned to myself.

What could *I* do for me? How did I bring this condition into being? Did I still need it? What was it teaching me? How could I better cooperate with my body? When I "fell into the hole in my back" and screamed in agony, unable to move, was I actually slipping in consciousness, not living up to my highest and best?

I spent months practicing deep breathing into the weak area to strengthen it with my presence. I taught myself how to pull up on my spine and align my vertebrae. I focused on responding freely in my whole being during moments of emergency rather than grabbing hold in my lower back.

I was determined to bring change into being.

I refused to give myself over to aspirin or Darvon. I would not depend on a brace or an outside support system when I was fully capable of supporting myself.

It wasn't the fault of the doctors that they couldn't do anything for my condition other than prescribe pain killers. As a matter of fact, that they could do nothing was their gift to me. It was for *me* to do something for me, since it was *me* who had done it *to* me!

I healed my back by healing what had hurt my back in the first place. For almost two years now I have been free of pain. Hallelujah!

I have the capacity to heal myself in every way So do you—by *being* the change you want to see happen. It's up to you to give yourself the opportunity to heal yourself. Ask yourself what you need. If it's a cleansing of toxins and excess residues, give your body the gift of a water fast or a change in diet. There are many excellent books to guide you along this course. If you want time to journey inward and focus on your needs, give it to yourself. Only *you* can. Only you can *be* the change.

When you are being the change you want to see happen, you are functioning from your Higher Self; you are choosing to respond actively to your dis-ease rather than haphazardly *re*acting.

As you focus on rebirth, focus on laughter, focus on humor, focus on joy. The more seriously you take your condition, the more serious your condition will be.

Laugh at yourself. Laugh at your condition. Laughter reverberates through your body; it rejuvenates your cells and shakes up coagulated masses of dis-ease. There is humor and joy in all things. Look for it, reflect it.

If the change you want to see happen is to have fun again, begin by making fun of your condition, by having fun with it.

If you want to move out of darkness, make *light* of what troubles you.

What I'm telling you is not a game; I'm not playing with words. A change of attitude is the beginning to bringing change into being.

Change will become a reality if you are being it.

10

TO BE OR NOT TO BE... IT'S A MATTER OF CHOICE

This chapter is a love gift for you if you have ever contemplated, or are now contemplating, suicide.

There is pain, and there is pain that goes beyond pain. There is pain that is so loud that it deafens you to any of the other sounds of life. There is pain so sharp that it fills the eyes with constant tears that blind. There is pain so deep, so cutting, that it seems to tear to bloody shreds the inner fibers of your being.

That is the pain beyond pain. It is so powerful that it evokes the agonizing cry, "I can't go on. I can't take any more. I won't do it any longer." When the last strain of the cry fades into the outer reaches of the galaxy, deadened silence remains—the sound of nothing. In the nothing, the notion of suicide is introduced as a viable possibility. It is, after all, a way out. It *is* an answer. It *is* an ending.

I walked in the deadened silence. I know. I was nineteen years old and I had been through the pain that goes beyond pain. I was lonely, love-starved, panicked by the thought of risking, afraid of the strength of my own being. I couldn't find my identity; I didn't know where I was heading; I didn't know whom to ask for help, how to ask for it, or even that I *could* ask.

I was a counselor in a summer camp and the beauty of nature that surrounded me revolted me because it so profoundly pointed up what I saw as my ugliness. I couldn't take any more. The next day was my day off. I hitchhiked into town and spent hours walking alone. The streets were grey and empty, or maybe I was. Late in the afternoon I bought a bottle of vodka. What was strange about the purchase was that it didn't feel odd to me to be doing it, even though it was totally out of character. I'd never bought liquor before. I didn't drink. By the time I left the store, my plan of action had taken its full shape. Ironically, the anticipation of the suicide became the purpose of my life—the purpose which had been missing in my life, and which had led me to this moment.

I hitched back to camp, talking with the driver as if this were just any other day. Little did he know. Little did anyone know. I hoped they would all feel sorry when they found my body. It sounds silly and childish to talk about this aspect of it now, and yet, that is highly appropriate in that it *is* the little self who commits suicide. It's the feeling self that can't take any more and shuts down completely, eventually killing the body in the process.

Around six in the evening I went down near the lake. For the next three hours, on an empty stomach, I drank straight vodka from the bottle. It tasted terrible. I hated it. I felt myself getting sicker and sicker and losing touch with my senses. I almost reached the point of disbanding the suicide plan. This is the crucial point you reach when the way you are trying to kill yourself feels worse to you than what led you to the attempt to begin with. I almost reached that point, but I didn't.

At about nine o'clock, feeling sick to my stomach and disgusted, I stood up and walked (or reeled) to the edge of the dock. I engaged in a long series of reflections about the family and friends who never gave me what I wanted or needed. (I hadn't asked, but that didn't occur to me then.) I wasn't being overly dramatic about my deprivations, just deeply sad and unprepared to deal with any of it any more. I had moved beyond reality into a limbo in which I would never have to deal with anything again—impending death.

I looked down into the deep water and prepared to jump. In that moment my re-mind gave me an incredible gift. It shot me the thought, "Hey, I can't swim! What the hell am I doing here? I could drown!" I turned and ran from the water's edge, sobbing hysterically as I dashed my body through branches and thickets. In the moment when I could see what I was *actually* planning to do, I couldn't go through with it. I had *thought* I wanted to die, but I *knew* I didn't want to drown! It was only while I was blinded to the larger picture that my Higher Self had to offer me, that I could allow one facet of myself, little self, to kill the rest of me.

My mind had shaken me to my rational senses by asking a perfectly simple and truthful question. So incredible was the question that my little self was jolted into responding. Little self let loose with fears and tears. The feelings flowed, thus releasing the seemingly sole alternative—death. Little self wanted to die because the fear and the tears were so bound up inside as to cause inner suffocation of the self, and the death of both little self and body. When what was held was released, the very substance that had led to suicide led to new life.

The contemplation of suicide, then, can be a life-saver rather than a destroyer. In wanting to kill self, you are wanting to rid yourself of the stuck place you have created in yourself which is in fact killing you! No wonder you can't take it any more. And since you're the one who is creating the reality in the first place, you can simply stop and start again.

There's another thing about suicide that makes a successful attempt an act of futility. It offers you no guarantees. How do you know but that once you end it all, there won't be more? How do you know but that you won't have to deal with the same problem all over again, another time around?

Listen to the phrase *to take your own life*. It sounds like an incomplete sentence to me. To take your life where? And if *you* take your life somewhere, aren't *you* still ongoing and therefore still dealing with the energy configuration with which you had surrounded your self? Unfinished business clings; unfinished energy configurations reconstitute themselves.

If you don't believe in reincarnation or in timeless, continuous life, perhaps it's all the more reason to take another look at your plan to finish yourself altogether. If this is all there is, is this *all* you really want to do with it? Can you be that sure? Perhaps you could ask yourself another question. Is this your very best? I'll give you a way to measure it. Would you be doing this if you were well and happy? "No!" you say? "Ridiculous question!" you say? Not any more ridiculous than making so momentous a decision as suicide at one of the lowest points in your life. Seriously, in order to really know for sure that this is the only choice left to you, at least wait until you can acknowledge that the sun is shining *on* you.

What's that you're saying? It isn't fair to say this because I know damn well that under those circumstances you wouldn't be getting ready to do this? Well, if that's the case, maybe it would be well for *you* to listen to what you're saying. Before you cash in your chips and remove your options, the least you can do is play fairly and give yourself every chance.

One way to give yourself a new perspective is to close your eyes and imagine the entire suicide exactly as if it were actually happening. Let yourself see it all and do it all on your inner TV screen. Walking to the pills. Opening the bottle. Or, going to the medicine chest, taking out the razor, and rolling up your sleeves. Or, opening the window and bringing your leg up to the sill in order to bring your body out to the ledge. (If you find, by the way, that you can't handle the imagining, perhaps suicide is not really what you want to do. It's just a thought.)

Complete your imagining, that is, when you've downed the pills one after another and you feel sick to your stomach and begin to lose consciousness and you see yourself lying on the bed losing color and you experience your vital organs collapse one by one. Or, when you've sliced the razor into the vulnerable flesh and veins of your wrists and you watch your life blood flowing out of your body and onto the bathroom floor. Or, well, you do your own imagining. Make it terrible, because that's what violence to self is. Make it the worst you can envision, because that is what it will be like, and because that's what will constitute success.

Be sure not to simply damage yourself. Be sure that you die in your imagery. A terrible possibility in suicides is surviving them and having to deal, perhaps for the rest of your life, with the injuries inflicted on self, which might be far worse than the pain you experienced prior to the attempt.

When you've finished your imagining and have "died," see what you see. Do you see relief? Do you see bliss, an end to your troubles? If you do, *who* is seeing this? If it's *you*, then the suicide didn't really work because *you* are still left to deal with what you left behind and tried to murder. If there's nothing when you finish with your imagining, if the TV screen simply goes blank, turn it off. Get up and walk out of that inner room just as you do when a show is over. (Even if you've found bliss and see that *you* really do go on, do the same thing. Turn off the set and leave the room.) Pick up the threads of life and start living *as if* you had actually killed yourself and had erased all that had preceded this moment. Allow your life to simply begin, as of this *very* moment.

This can be an ongoing process. When you go to sleep each night, die to the day that has just passed and in the morning, awake newly born to the new day and the vast possibilities that await you. It's a way of having your suicide and living beyond it too!

There *is* pain that goes beyond pain. There is *also* new life that waits beyond the pain that goes beyond pain. Killing self out of desperation is hardly your best shot. Killing yourself because you have completely given in to one facet of yourself (your body and its pain, your little self and its hurt) is like throwing the baby out with the bath water.

If you really want to die, live like the dickens and let nature take its course. You'd be surprised how well the universe has your life in hand and knows what's best for you. Discover what that is by sticking with it.

If you simply can't wait, can't hack it, don't want to live, then go to it. Take your life. Take it wherever you need to and deal with what's going on with you *there*.

In the beginning you were given yourself. Make sure you are in good hands. Only you can know.

11

FROM TERMINAL TO TRANSITIONAL

This chapter is for those of you who are living haphazardly, and especially for those of you who have been given the "unmentionable" prognosis. Have you been told that you are going to die? The very sentence itself creates a lump in the throat. What a thing to have to deal with. It's no joke. It's not easy for you. It's not easy for those who share life with you. It's something to shout at. "It's unfair." "I don't want to die." "Oh, God!" "Why me?" Whatever you want to say about it, I'm with you. To be finished before you're finished is heavy.

The truth is, however, that you are not alone. *We are all going to die!* Perhaps that didn't really occur to you prior to your condition. Did you ever catch yourself saying, "*If* I die . . ." instead of, "*When* I die . . ."?

We are all dying. The difference between you

and others is that *you* have now allowed that awareness into your consciousness, and you may know approximately *when* you are going to die. Did it ever occur to you to delight in this knowledge? To be grateful rather than choosing to be incapacitated by it? Not many of us have such inside information. Most of us want to go on living in this form a while longer; not all of us can. Many of us say, "I don't want to die." You might want to change your reality by saying instead, "I don't want to die until . . ." or, "I want to live."

If your objective is to live and your days are numbered (and all of our days are numbered!) —to such an extent that you have actually been given the count—then *live*. Live every single moment to the fullest of your ability. Be conscious all the time. Take care of all those things you want to do *before you die*. If your objective is to live, then die wide awake, without drugs that rob you of your precious awareness; die without machines that make you one of them. Die with dignity and you will have lived a very long life, regardless of the number of years.

It would be well for all of us, whether we've been told when or not, to live as if each day were the very last we had. If we did, we'd spend our very precious time doing only what was essential, meaningful, and joyful. We'd never take anyone or anything for granted. We'd invest our energy in rejoicing rather than complaining. We'd quickly take care of any unfinished business and render ourselves up-to-date.

What about you, my friend? You who have been told that you are going to die. Have you been spending your precious time in despair, ruing the verdict? Or are you filling each moment with beauty and joy? Is there anyone in your life to whom you've meant to say something that has gone unsaid? Anyone you need to forgive, or from whom you need to ask forgiveness? Anyone you meant to thank, to tell how much you've loved? Is there anyone for whom you can do something or from whom you can receive something? Don't be a dangling participle in life. Live whole and go whole.

Use your time to acquaint yourself with death. Preparing for it is merely a speeded-up version of living. What I mean is that so many of us, alas, take life for granted. We let it live us instead of living *it*, consciously. There's no hurry, we say. There's tomorrow and tomorrow, and next week. There's plenty of time to fathom life. That is, until we are told of our impending death, or we become aware that each day we are living, we are also dying. The awareness of death forces us to look at life more fully and to look at death as well. After all, we feel more comfortable going into something new when we have some idea of what it's about.

Have you thought about it? Do you know what death is? Do you buy the terminology *terminal illness?* That's purely a medical term, you know. The medical profession, while focused, and admirably, to be sure, on saving lives, is actually engaged in saving bodies. The distinction is vitally important.

A terminal illness means that the body will not survive the effects of the dis-ease. This has little to do with you. *You* will not be terminated. You are *not* your body, remember? Terminal has only to do with what is temporal. Terminal has only to do with the impending death of the flesh.

A far more appropriate term is *transitional illness,* indicating that what is the cause of death in the body is simultaneously the new coming into being and altering the state of the soul (the spirit, the you, who continues). Death then, is a rebirth in which life goes on in a form which does not express itself through the body. Death is the stage beyond helplessness, beyond limitations, beyond hopelessness. Death is the next phase.

The phrase life-*after*-death is confusing. In fact, there is life *in* death. Death is a time of transition, not of ending and new beginning. How do *I* know? I've experienced it. I recalled a time of life in another body. I was more frightened of death than anything imaginable. I was convinced it was the end of everything and I couldn't deal with that. As it turned out, the joke was on me. The hardest part of dying (or shifting to the new stage of consciousness) was living through my self-created fears and doubts and letting go of my hold on what I thought was the only way one could live—namely, through the body. When I let go, when I let the body die, I actually saw the body. Therein lay the joke. *I* was looking at the "deceased me." I hadn't terminated, I had transitioned!

The process of recalling "past lives" is a relatively simple one in which to engage. The first step is to know that it is indeed *possible* for you to have a recall. If you say that it is impossible, it will be. If you say, "This is pure nonsense," then any memory you might bring into focus by accident will make *no sense* to you and you will pay little attention to it. If you allow yourself to *know* that recalls are possible, then you do two things immediately. First, you acknowledge that you haven't *yet* had one. Second, that you're open to the possibility of having one.

Step two is to *want* to have a recall. Not to *push* for it, but to welcome it and actively seek it by remaining open and thus making yourself conscious of the clues being presented to you if and as they emerge.

Step three can be done alone or with a helper. It is the step known as consciousness shifting, or in reincarnation recall terminology, regression. Both terms means the same thing. However, for me the former is a broader and more inclusive concept than the latter. Regression is highly specific. It refers to moving back to other lives, other periods of consciousness. On the other hand, consciousness shifting includes not only the possibility of regression but also level-shifting between planes of consciousness without necessarily experiencing a recall. Hence, while regression is goal-oriented, consciousness shifting is free form (free of form).

Doing the shifting by yourself is easy if you know what you are doing. It's mostly a matter of stilling the body, breathing deeply and moving consciously into Higher Self and beyond. Once in this state beyond thought and feeling, you can relinquish your body (your formedness) and ask your Higher Self to take you on whatever journey into inner self or expanded self it might like at this point in timelessness. Then, just go and register the journey along the way.

Past lives will present themselves in living color. You will see your self of then in time, place, body, clothing, etc. You might hear yourself in another language. You will feel what you felt then and think what you thought then.

Of course, you might not have any recall. It may be that this is your first time around or that what you are working on now does not necessitate the remembering of previous life experiences.

You might simply experience other levels or planes of consciousness. You might come face to face with the larger-than-personality-self of you and look back at your personality self and see it sitting, seeing you! You might move into the radiant void in which you are nothing, in which *you* do not exist. You might come to know that simultaneously you are all there is—you *are* the universe—that you are everyone who ever lived and ever *will* live.

If you don't know what I'm talking about, simply acknowledge that you don't know *yet,* that there's more than you've ever dreamed of, that there's always more.

If you've created the reality that this simple

process is too complicated for you, or impossible for you to accomplish, you might want to seek out the services of someone who specializes in level shifting or recall.

My first experience of shifting was on my own. I looked into a flower, relinquished the form I was seeing with my physical eyes and instantly experienced the energy of (the energy which was) the flower. I saw the energy moving in and through itself in waves and bands. I moved on from there to see it in other things, in anything that masquerades as substance, from human bodies to stone walls, to water. I have learned how to choose simply to shift my consciousness and see beyond the form. As a result, I know that that is all that death is—a shift from form to formless energy in a continuation of life.

As for recalls, though I also have those spontaneously on my own, I began by enlisting the services of helpers. The team I worked with relaxed me and invited me to journey back through time. I felt myself diving into nothingness, sinking lower and lower as if being submerged in the earth of life in order that I might see my roots as well as what had flowered.

As I passed below the level of what had previously been in my range of consciousness, I experienced extreme cold throughout my physical body. The cold and chills persisted even after I was covered with several blankets.

I was not afraid. I wanted to go deeper. I wanted to know. After a while, the inner screen began to play old movies. I saw myself, my energy, in other forms.

Perhaps the real fear of death is the fear of the fear of death. Perhaps the phrase "I'm scared to death" grew out of the realization that so many of us bring ourselves to the doorstep or the consciousness of death scared. We tremble and pull back and create a block to moving on with the new. In the Bible the word fear conveys a sense of awe. A transition to another plane of consciousness does indeed induce a sense of awe and wonder. If we proceed in fear, in lack of trust, we pull back and make the transition a trial. If we proceed in wonder, in awe, in reverence, we open ourselves fully and render ourselves divinely aware as we make the transition.

Each of us has experienced the transitional dimension of death, though we call it by another name. It is birth. Generally, as little is known of it as is known of its counterpart, death. From this plane of consciousness, a plane of form and matter, we perceive birth and death as in and out. We are born *into* the body, and that is praiseworthy because we can see, touch, and experience the form. We die by going out of the body, and we don't like that because we lose our sensuous experience of the representation of the person.

In truth, birth is a transition in individual consciousness from non-form to form, and death is the transition from form to non-form. We've all been there. We never really leave where we've come from.

We bring the consciousness with us when we manifest, and take it with us when we move on. It is our degree of awareness that differs.

If you remember your moment of birth, you will find the moment of death much easier to anticipate. If you remember the moment of conception, when the universal you began to crystallize into the material you (the matter and personality), the moment of death, the return to being all and nothing simultaneously, the journey back to the Father's house, will be a moment of joy.

Dying is a time which calls for your active participation in the process. Prepare yourself for the shift in consciousness that will occur; know what is taking place in you as it happens. Read the experiences of others. Seek out someone who can be with you while you make the transition represented by death; who can talk with you as you cross over, who can journey part of the way with you. Share the ecstasy and illumination of your death with a loved one, just as you shared the incredible joy of your birth with one or both of your parents.

Does ecstasy seem an inappropriate word to be used in relation to death? Then at least be comforted that there are persons in the world who know death to be ecstasy. What can be true for others can be true for you. If death is an unknown to you because of your current lack of awareness and personal experience, it will *become* known when you die. Why be frightened in advance of the unknown? When it becomes known, it might not be frightening at all.

If you create unnecessary fear now the joke will be on you later when you encounter the bliss.

Living is not wasting a moment. Be the highest and best you can be in the time-space that remains to you. If your objective is to live, you can. Inevitable death is not your obstacle; you are. Get out of your way.

12

BEYOND THE CONDITION

In the beginning I told you that whenever you heard what I was saying, it would be because I was the echo of your own inner voice. I have delighted in sounding thought-provoking, growth-producing tones for you. I spoke with you in the chamber of your larger self—the energy aura surrounding your physical body. I am preparing now to move out of your sphere. You no longer need the echo. You can hear your own inner voice directly. You have met your own Higher Self, heeded your own knowing and wisdom. You have called on your own strength for your own healing. That has been my purpose, to introduce you to yourself. I can leave you in no better hands.

Lest you think you are finished when your condition of dis-ease is pronounced officially over and done with, I want to leave you with some thoughts to seriously ponder as you make your first moves into the world of being fully well.

You have lived and grown with and through the dis-ease; can you now *live* without it? By *live,* I mean *consciously live.*

The dis-ease stimulated you to new awareness, it demanded that you be alert to what your various facets of self were telling you. It insisted that you make changes, let go of old habits and attitudes, make major shifts in the way you approached the process of living. It forced you to live consciously rather than haphazardly.

Can you now, without the dis-ease to nag you, continue to live in the same consciousness? Or will you need to create another dis-ease, and then another, to keep forcing yourself to hear your own voice?

It is imperative that during your time of good health, you be awake to all the choices you are making. Metaphorically speaking, you will be working life's knitting needles, producing the garments your soul will be wearing in the world. If you slip in your consciousness, you will drop a stitch, then another, and another. Each one will be a point of weakness in your garment. Over a period of time, those points of weakness begin to pull apart. You are left with gaping holes, passageways inviting dis-ease to take up residence.

Your task during the illness was to become aware of what you, the teacher, wanted to impart to you, the student of evolving life.

You do not need to shake yourself to a breaking

point to move off an old center and onto a new one. You need only to make new choices. Making choices means constant activation of the Higher Self. It means monitoring your thoughts, feelings, and bodily sensations. It means taking frequent inventory of your life—cleaning out what you no longer need, bringing in what is required.

If you are lonely, do not invest energy in trying to convince yourself that:

You are not
You don't need anybody
It's a sign of weakness
You have to grin and bear it
So is everyone else
That's the way life is

If you are lonely, *do* something about it. Begin by acknowledging that you are. Register it clearly in your Higher Self. "I am lonely. That is what is going on with me, right now." Then ask yourself, your little self, what you want to do about that loneliness. Does your body need to be held? Can you hold it, or do you need others to wrap you in their arms? Are you willing to ask for what you need? Is there someone you can ask? Is there no one? Is there someone you are overlooking? Is there someone you assume would refuse who might well oblige? Are you fully providing others with the opportunities to give to you? Are you doing so while having no expectations of how that person will respond, taking care not to set yourself up for disappointment?

Do you need time to rest? Are you taking it?

Are you offering yourself all kinds of reasons for not taking it? Do you receive yourself as beautiful only when you are pushing yourself *beyond* your capacity? Are you willing to receive yourself as beautiful when you can go no further, when you need to quit, when you need to lie down? Are you willing to ask for help?

Listen to yourself! Give yourself what you need and you'll move beyond that need. Live in Higher Self and you'll live in awareness of what is transpiring in you. Living in Higher Self when there is no dis-ease to draw your attention, is the real test of what you have learned thus far.

Living in Higher Self is equivalent to living in love. It is keeping all the channels clear and unblocked; allowing life energy to flow through you uninhibited, unsnagged. Living in love is expressing gratitude for all things, especially those you do not want or understand.

When you were stricken, did you perchance say, in a hushed whisper that only God could hear, "Just let me get through this and I'll never be bad again," (or something like that)? If you said it, you were offering to live out of your highest and best self upon recovery. That's an easy offer to make when you are lying at the bottom of the pile. The tendency is to forget it when you are on your feet again.

That's the prize-fight of life. You swing as if you had forever when you're standing on your feet, and you beg, plead, and promise when you've been knocked on your bottom.

The secret is to live out of Higher Self when you are normal and healthy. If you do it when you are down, you can pick yourself up. If you do it when you're up, you can lift yourself into a realm in which there exists a never ending high, one which moves into ever greater bliss.

The high is such that you no longer need to create a downer for yourself in order to experience contrasting energies, in order to have a base to move up and on from. The high serves as the springboard to the higher still.

Let's focus on your hands as a simple example of the process I am referring to.

The hands, under ordinary circumstances, might be regarded with gratitude in the rare moment when the owner takes notice of them. He is grateful that he has them, that they work well, that he can do all the things he can do because of them. How often have you taken a moment to express gratitude for your hands? Constantly? Every hour? Once a day? Once a week? Once a year? Once in the last ten years?

And then, think of all the other parts of your body. If you spent time being grateful for all of them, you would spend your entire life being grateful. And *that is the point,* you see. You *can* make of your life a constant expression of gratitude and *never* run out of things to be grateful for. The shift into such a mode of living is a shift into ecstasy.

Let us return to the hands for a moment so that we might fully trace the course from being down, to being up, to being beyond both.

During normal living, the hands are taken for granted. Because there's hardly a move you make without them, they merge into a larger whole and fade from your consciousness. Enter the down period: Your hands are stricken with arthritis. You cannot move the joints, your fingers are crippled. You cannot write, or hold objects, or comb your hair. You are in terrible pain.

Now comes the whisper: "Please return the use of my hands and I'll never take them for granted again."

Enter healing: With it comes the move from despair to delight along a very fickle path. From down to up is little more than a seesaw. The measure of the high and low is fixed. It goes no lower; it goes no higher. Either one or the other is at the mercy of the weight of focus which you use to tip the scales. The hands are sometimes thought of, sometimes forgotten.

A child's swing is a good metaphor for the journey into ever greater bliss. You begin by sitting with your feet already off the ground. You are suspended in joy over the marvel of the hands which serve you so well. Each time you swing, you express gratitude and love for your blessing. The curve grows longer with each thrust forward until you have formed a semi-circle in the air. With your head flung back, you are in bliss. The circle is completed by the arc in the cosmos which unites with yours in ecstasy.

Throughout it all, you are extolling the glory of your hands. You are conscious of what they can do, how they move, what they can hold, how they respond to your wishes, how beautiful they look, how wonderfully they are shaped, how unique they are to your body, how strong they are, how flexible, how they touch, how they feel sensations, how they create. The list is unending, just as the high is topless.

There is only more and more over which to marvel. The greater your will to do it, the less your need will be to drag yourself into dis-ease in order to appreciate what you have.

There is one more thing you should know. It is one of the great paradoxes of life. The more consistent the state of high, the greater the degree of consciousness, the greater the susceptibility to new dis-ease.

As the high expands and the consciousness deepens, the vibration in which you live becomes finer, purer. While this opens the way for you to tap levels of knowing hitherto unexposed to you, you are much more susceptible to registering all that is taking place in and around you.

Perhaps it would be easier if I compared the process to an electric fan. When it is not turned on, you can see the individual blades in their still position. There is little risk of anything going wrong with the fan when it is not in use. When you utilize almost nothing of your awareness, not much happens to and through you either.

The shift from downer to high can be seen when the fan is switched on low. You can see the blades moving, and you can see the spaces in between, linked to the blades by moving vibrations. Plugged in, turned on, in operation, you and the fan are open to possible junctures of stuckness or disease. Simultaneously you are moving and flowing. You can both sense your power of being and the energy moving through you. Electricity in the fan, or consciousness in you, is required to keep the operation running smoothly. Any short in the current opens the way for dis-ease and readjustment in the mechanism is required.

When the fan is turned to high, the speed is so great that the fan blades are no longer visible and the view through to the other side is transparent. The same is true when your sensitivity is so heightened that no barrier exists between you and the expanded planes of consciousness that you have rendered yourself capable of knowing. You are open to everything. Because you have lightened the matter consistency of your vibrational field, your responses to events in the environment around you come much more quickly into manifestation, just as the fast-moving fan can in an instant sever or shred whatever comes into its sphere.

If, for example, you refuse to shed tears, they will instantly take the form of congestion in your eyes or sinuses. From suppression to head cold in one easy step. In the past, prior to your greater sensitivity, you would have been more able to absorb the suppressed fears into the thickness of the vibrational field with which you were choosing to surround yourself. When molecules can join already coagulated matter, it is not necessary to bring new shapes and forms into being. The reverse is also true. The finer the vibration in which you live, the more quickly the very slightest disharmony will register and take up form and residence in some part of your psyche.

If spontaneous combustion and instantaneous manifestations are more than you wish to handle at this time, you can desert your pyramid of consciousness. Weeds, like shadows, will grow over the stones of your knowing and years or ages from now, on an archeological expedition into self, you may have cause to wonder why you abandoned the brilliant edifice of knowing that you built. Perhaps then you will be ready to uncover once more the startling power of transparent vibrations.

As for now, hold in your awareness only that which will not overload your circuits. Blowing fuses only causes static in the universe.

13

WHY ME?

We have shared a great deal together, you and I —I with you and you with yourself. The latter is the most important. What I, or anyone else, shares with you becomes relevant only when it is received by you, absorbed by you, translated by you, and put to use for you and by you.

You have asked, "Why me?" The asking was in order that you might explore the wide variety of answers to that question and thereby activate the healing process in yourself, bringing the condition you had created into greater harmony with the larger whole of you.

Each time a "Why me?" rears its head in you, answer it with a specific "Because." The Love Project principles are very helpful in formulating "because" statements that are profoundly significant. They can become a pathway to wholeness for the stricken.

Why me, you ask. And among the answers: Because I was the one who helped create this reality in myself! I may not have done so consciously, but I participated in the creation nonetheless. Knowing that I played an important role in the creation of the dis-ease, I can now play an equally important role in bringing the new, the healing, the harmonious, into being—this time consciously. Why me? Because I'm the one who did it to myself. Why me? Because I'm capable of handling whatever it is I am stricken/blessed with.

Why me? Because I didn't receive myself (or someone else) as beautiful exactly where I was (they were). I was critical, judgmental, and condemnatory. I blocked my loveflow and hindered the intake and output of my energy. Why me? Because I was and am ready to open myself to life, to love, to the me of me, and to others. Why me? Because I needed to make myself aware of how critically I was congesting myself by setting up road blocks to incoming people-traffic. I am ready now to clear my energy highway and allow the life-force to flow in a steady stream.

Why me? Because I wasn't *being* the change I wanted to see happen. I wasn't even sure what change I *wanted* to see happen. I took no positive action in any new direction. I made myself a victim and waited around for others to do something for me, or for life to change. Why me? Because I wasn't holding on to the reins of my life and, hence, the horsepower that could have been directed toward effecting change was instead set loose on the track, riderless and wild. Why me? Because it's time for me to take charge. My spirit is champing at the bit, waiting for me to lead the way. It's time for me to evaluate the changes I want to see happen in my life and in my dis-ease, and to bring those changes into being *by being* them.

Why me? Because I was trapped in a problem-orientation to life. It was imperative I be stricken severely in order that I might come to know that every seeming problem is an opportunity. Why me? Because I was rigid in my old approaches to life and saw any new possibility as a threat.

I needed to break loose, to untie my holds on the past, to learn to welcome change. Why me? Because I was in need of perceiving the opportunity in *all* life experience. Why me? Because I am worthy of being challenged to move off the base of status quo to the tower of limitlessness in which no bounds exist. Why me? Because it takes something profound to make me see something profound.

Why me? Because I was a do-it-yourselfer. I was selfish. I didn't provide others with the opportunity to give to me. I closed myself off instead. I couldn't receive because I couldn't really give. To receive from another is to truly give that other a great gift. Why me? Because I didn't feel worthy of receiving, because I felt an obligation if I received; because I didn't know how to ask for what I needed or wanted. Why me? Because I needed to be knocked flat, to be placed in a state of vulnerability, in order that I might learn how to provide others with the opportunity to give to me.

Why me? Because I was laden with expectations; hence I was constantly being disappointed. Why me? Because I needed to learn about setting goals with open-ended means of achieving them. Because it was important for me to leave behind me the philosophy known as "the only way." There are many ways and they blossom when I'm living in abundant expectancy. Why me? Because I had to let go (in re-mind and little self) and let God (let my Higher Self) take over.

Why me? Because I needed to take a look at the way I was living my life and make some new choices about how to proceed. I had neglected my choice-making duties. As a citizen living in the land of my body, I must fulfill my responsibility and make sure that my re-mind, my little self, and my physical self are given equal representation, and that their input is administered with care by my Higher Self—the seat of my choice-making. Why me? Because *only* I can do anything for me.

I'm not much for saying goodbye. It would hardly be appropriate in this case, since I have been the echo of your own inner voice and that never does leave you.

Rather, let me paraphrase a line from the Bible, "Hear, O Israel, the Lord our God is one." Hear, O friend of mine, the voice of your many facets is one. Listen to it well. It will serve in times of need and more importantly in times of no need, when you are reaching beyond the limitations of now into the vastness of all that lies before you and in you.

Why *you?* Why *not* you?

Perhaps the next time you ask, "Why me?" you will be able to answer yourself clearly, swiftly, profoundly.

When you can say, "I *know* why me," you will no longer be stricken, and therefore no longer hurt.

I love you. Please do the same.

APPENDIX

Thank you for letting me share with you. I would be delighted to have you share with me as well. If this book has been of help to you, write and tell me how. I'd really like to know. You can reach me at P.O. Box 7601, San Diego, California 92107.

I'd also like to meet you. Perhaps you would like to explore the healing-growing-evolving process further in one of our Love Project Practice Sessions (in Self-Healing, in Creating Your Own Reality Consciously, in Channeling Love Energy, in Re-Viewing Your Past, etc.). That would be wonderful. If you write and ask for one, I will send you a schedule of our sharings in various parts of the country and of Journeys Into Self to various parts of the world. You might like to take part in one of our sessions.

The Love Project is a way of life, not an organization. But Diane Pike and I act as a communications link for persons throughout the country and the world who are practicing being more loving by applying the six Love Project principles in their lives.

If you write, I'll also send you a sample of the *Seeker Newsletter,* a small magazine filled with articles and letters from persons around the world who are seeking to be more loving. And I will send you detailed descriptions of several books that might be of further help to you in your continuing exploration and healing of self.

BIBLIOGRAPHY

Bragg, Paul C. *The Miracle of Fasting*. Burbank, Ca.: Health Science, 1923.

Keyes, Laurel Elizabeth. *Toning: The Creative Power of the Voice*. Marina del Rey, Ca.: DeVorss & Co., 1976.

Lorrance, Arleen. *The Love Project*. San Diego, Ca.: LP Publications, 1972.

———, *Buddha from Brooklyn*. San Diego, Ca.: LP Publications, 1975.

———, *Musings for Meditation*. San Diego, Ca.: LP Publications, 1976.

———, with Pike, Diane K., *Channeling Love Energy*. San Diego, Ca.: LP Publications, Revised Edition, 1976.

Pike, Diane Kennedy. *Life Is Victorious! How to Grow through Grief*. New York: Simon and Schuster, 1976.

INDEX